Contents

About the authors

Vee P Prasher MB, ChB, MMedSc, MRCPsych, MD, PhD

Dr Vee Prasher is a Consultant Psychiatrist and Associate Professor of Neuro-developmental Psychiatry in Birmingham, UK. He has an internationally recognised reputation in the field having published over 100 articles on many aspects of physical and psychological problems in adults with Down syndrome. He has completed several post-doctorate degrees (MMedSc, MD, PhD) highlighting important health issues for people with Down syndrome. Vee Prasher has clinical responsibility for a large number of adults with a learning disability in the West Midlands and teaching and research responsibilities in the Department of Psychiatry, University of Birmingham. At present Vee Prasher is involved in a number of international research studies investigating the treatment and prevention of Alzheimer's disease in adults with Down syndrome.

Beryl Smith BSc, Dip Ed Psych, PhD

Beryl Smith has worked in the field of learning disability with both children and adults for 34 years, as educational psychologist, researcher, teacher trainer and university lecturer. During the 1990s she set up a master's course for professionals working with adults with a learning disability in the community. She has now retired and is editor of *The SLD Experience*, a journal published by BILD for parents and practitioners working with and caring for children and young people with severe learning difficulties.

ACKNOWLEDGEMENTS

Our thanks to all the people with Down syndrome, their families and numerous professionals in the West Midlands, who allowed us to spend time with them to collect information for this book.

Better Healthcare For Adults with Down Syndrome

British Library Cataloguing in Publication Data

A CIP record for this book is available from the Public Library

ISBN 1 902519 205

BILD Publications is the publishing office of the
British Institute of Learning Disabilities
Campion House
Green Street
Kidderminster
Worcs
DY10 1JL

Telephone: 01562 723010
Fax: 01562 723029
e-mail: enquiries@bild.org.uk
Website: www.bild.org.uk

Please contact BILD for a free publications catalogue listing BILD books, reports and training materials.

Thanks to The Down's Syndrome Association for funding an early study which was the basis for the book. Thanks also to many professional colleagues for their valuable comments on the differing chapters: Dr A Sharma, Wordsley Hospital; Dr C. Dyer, Mr I Donaldson, Dr J Winer and Dr E. Rankin, University Hospital; Dr N Gittoes and Dr M Huengsberg, University of Birmingham; B. Quirke, Derbyshire Dental Department. Thanks to Brian Bryne and Ann Cody for the original illustrations. Thanks finally to Professor John Harris and to Alison Wall, British Institute of Learning Disabilities, for their valuable comments on earlier versions of this manuscript.

Preface

This book has been written to promote better understanding of the healthcare needs of adults with Down syndrome. Many books are already available giving general information to families of children with Down syndrome, with more specialised medical textbooks available to clinicians and academics regarding disorders in adults with the syndrome.

There is, however, a need for a book giving simple, basic, practical information on aspects of health problems that an adult with Down syndrome may experience during his or her lifetime. This book aims to meet that need.

As the vast majority of adults with Down syndrome now live in the community it is vital that families and carers are made aware of all aspects of problems in health that can occur. Professionals in the Health Service are not always fully aware of the healthcare needs of people with a learning disability and this situation needs to be re-addressed. The up-to-date and practical information presented in this book will be of help to professionals, carers and families. It deals with both minor and more serious problems, their possible causes and how they should be treated and prevented. It aims to improve awareness of the most important physical and psychological problems encountered among adults with Down syndrome.

The book does not aim to give detailed medical information on all aspects of health in adults with Down syndrome. Rather, it gives an overview of the most common and the most important health concerns faced by professionals, families and carers. The book cannot replace a medical assessment but aims to improve care for adults with Down syndrome by suggesting ways in which families and carers can manage minor problems and alert health care professionals to more serious problems. **Various treatments are listed**

which can be used to treat a condition, but carers are advised to consult their GP if there are ongoing concerns.

How to use this book

The book is divided into three parts. The first part 'Personal and Social Issues' discusses general issues relating to good health for adults with Down syndrome. The second part 'Specific Medical Issues' focuses on health issues in defined areas. The third part 'Appendices and Resources' gives important sources of further support and information.

By turning to a particular chapter, readers can find information on the most significant conditions associated with that area of health. Alternatively, from the index, readers can be guided to the relevant condition.

Introduction

What are the important health issues for adults with Down syndrome?

While adults with Down syndrome are susceptible to the same range of medical problems as the general population, they are more likely to suffer from particular ailments. These include: heart problems, increased risk of hearing and vision loss, thyroid disease, skin problems, obesity and memory loss in older adults. Lack of appropriate medical care will impair an individual's level of social and intellectual functioning, dramatically affecting his or her quality of life. It may also have a significant impact on the well-being of families and carers. The treatment and prevention of secondary health problems are therefore of considerable importance, educationally and socially, as well as medically.

How great is the need for adults with Down syndrome to receive better healthcare?

Adults with Down syndrome are now living longer than previously, with many living into their 60s and 70s. For example, one person with Down syndrome has lived to the age of 78 years with no significant health problems. During the 20th century, the average life expectancy progressively increased from an estimated 9 years in 1929, to 12 years in 1947, to 18 years by 1961, to 30 years by 1973 and at the start of 21st century to 57 years of life. In the Western world 80% of children born recently with Down syndrome are expected to survive to the age of 5 years, 72% to the age of 30 years, 44% to the age of 60 years and 14% to 68 years.

With no significant fall in the birth rate of babies with Down syndrome (around one in every 1,000 births) and with adults with Down syndrome living longer, people with Down syndrome will, during the next few decades, become a significant proportion of the population. It is predicted that the number of people with Down syndrome in the UK will continue to rise, from 26,045 in 1981 to 27,459 in 2021. Between 1990 and 2010 the number of people with Down syndrome older than 40 years is expected to increase by about 75%, but the number of those aged 50 years or more will rise by about 200%. Such figures are likely to be an under-estimate, as many people with Down syndrome are not known to services. These findings demonstrate a slow but steady rise in the population of people with Down syndrome, for whom health remains an important issue.

Where should healthcare for adults with Down syndrome be targeted?

Until relatively recently, the care of adults with Down syndrome was largely institutional. Over the past 20 years, however, the move to care in the community for people with a learning disability has meant that the vast majority of adults with Down syndrome are now resettled in the community. Many live with their families, others live in statutory, voluntary or private community accommodation. A minority, usually older people, remain in the hospital setting. These changes mean that a focus on the provision of high quality care in the community is vital.

Who is responsible for healthcare provision?

The trend towards community care presents a major challenge to health and social services. This particularly applies to primary health care services where GPs are asked to look after an increased number of patients with a learning disability. However, GPs are often unaware of how many people with Down syndrome are on their lists, their associated physical and psychological conditions and of the different agencies involved in care provision. There remains, therefore, a considerable degree of unmet need.

Although no one would wish to go back in time and re-establish care in hospital for people with a learning disability, the move to care in the community has created a situation in which provision of appropriate health care presents a considerable challenge. In a hospital residential setting a wide range of health care services may be provided, such as regular medical examinations, physiotherapy, speech therapy, chiropody and provision and monitoring of drugs. Such a comprehensive network of health care may not be so readily available in the community.

For those people who live with elderly parents or relatives there is the additional problem that elderly carers may not recognise symptoms of ill-health or else consider them to be inevitably associated with the syndrome. Other barriers to obtaining health care may be difficulties in accessing transport, in using conventional appointment systems and waiting rooms and most importantly, the problem of communication between the person with a learning disability and the health care professional.

What role can families and carers play?

Healthcare for a person with Down syndrome begins at birth and possibly before birth. Parents and carers must be alert to medical complications that can occur throughout the life of a person with Down syndrome. Good healthcare provision based on prevention and early detection is essential for a high quality of life. With the introduction of community care, families and carers have an essential role to play in the provision of appropriate care for all people with Down syndrome.

Case studies

The level of service support required by adults with Down syndrome can vary from little more than infrequent routine screening to more acute immediate help. The following short case studies illustrate this:

Case 1

Stella is a young 26-year-old woman who has Down syndrome. She lives with her mother in their own home close to the city centre. Although Stella went to a school for children with special needs she left at 18 to work part-time in a nearby superstore. In the evenings she attends college and helps in a local youth centre. She is physically fit and well, needing only to wear glasses for short-sightedness. She maintains a healthy weight by dieting and regular exercise. "Mum laughs when I put my video on and jump up and down." Stella is able to read and write well, catch the bus to work on her own and is proud to admit: "It's not mum who looks after me, it's me who looks after mum." She thinks about having a boyfriend but says, "I've not met the right man yet!" She is taking no prescribed medication but is seen once a year by her doctor for a routine health-check.

Case 2

The complex needs of a person with Down syndrome are highlighted by the following story.

At the age of 48, John, a man with Down syndrome, was living in the family home, with his elderly mother aged 79 years. He had two sisters, both married with their own children and living away from home, but whom John saw on his birthday and at Christmas time. He enjoyed playing with his nephews and nieces.

When John was born his mother was told by the hospital staff "There's nothing we can do for you. Your son is a mongol and so will not live very long. You're better off putting him into an institution and getting on with your life. . ." Such advice was ignored and John's mother provided all care with little or no contact with health or social services until John, at the age of 47 years, was rushed to Casualty following what turned out to be a fit.

John recovered from his fit and was allowed home. His GP subsequently referred him to a Consultant Psychiatrist in Learning Disabilities. On assessment it was found that John had had a fall down the stairs six months earlier and was refusing to go up the stairs again, preferring to sleep on the couch downstairs. He had become housebound, refusing to leave the house or even walk in the garden. He was less able than a year previously, requiring more and more help from his mother to dress, wash, feed and to walk. He appeared to be unhappy and could be heard screaming out for no apparent reason. He had lost weight and at times was irritable towards his mother. Blood and urine tests revealed untreated hypothyroidism and a urinary tract infection. John made some improvement with thyroxine hormone replacement therapy and a course of antibiotics for the infection. During the next two months John had two further fits, became confused with evidence of impaired memory and was diagnosed as suffering from Alzheimer's disease – a particular form of dementia common in adults with Down syndrome.

His mother continued to provide care and initially refused to accept that she needed any form of help. She suffered from ill health herself. After several care reviews at the home she reluctantly accepted home help three days a week and community nurse support twice a week. Following further deterioration John had to be transferred to a Nursing Home. His mother received ongoing support throughout what became a traumatic time.

John's story demonstrates the importance of educating families, carers and professionals on the physical, psychological, social and family issues of health for all adults with Down syndrome.

PERSONAL AND SOCIAL ISSUES

Chapter 1

INTELLECTUAL, EMOTIONAL AND SOCIAL DEVELOPMENT

Intellectual and social development of children and adults with Down syndrome has in the past been generally neglected and ignored. Caring for people with Down syndrome used to be largely based on a model of care which often made the assumption that 'Down syndrome' was not a curable condition and therefore there was no point in trying to improve things.

Since the 1950s a more enlightened approach to supporting people has developed. It is now well recognised that intervention and stimulation can improve the level of both intellectual development and social competence or so called 'adaptive behaviour' (defined in terms of self-direction, responsibility and socialisation). This holistic approach to supporting individuals is an important factor in their development and growth as a person in their own right.

Intellectual functioning

The concept of the Intelligence Quotient (IQ) has had a considerable impact in defining level of intellectual ability. It can be calculated by using psychological tests, but results may be influenced by factors such as life experiences, the degree of co-operation, dexterity and anxiety of the person being tested. This makes accuracy uncertain, particularly for a person with a learning disability. Skilled use of appropriate IQ tests can be used to define the severity of a learning disability but nowadays what a person can do in terms of self-care and social skills is also considered important and is incorporated into defining the level of ability (Table 1).

Table 1: Levels of Learning Disability

Level of learning disability	Level of IQ	Level of social skills
Mild	50–69	good understanding and use of language, full independence in self-care skills, some help required with reading and writing, fully mobile
Moderate	35–49	limited language skills, supervision required with self-care, limited reading and writing skills, good mobility
Severe	20–34	marked impairment of language and communication, constant supervision required, poor reading and writing skills, usually limited mobility
Profound	less than 20	only basic understanding of communication, constant supervision required, no reading and writing skills, generally immobile

A level of IQ over 70 is defined as being in the 'normal' IQ range; the average IQ for the general population being 100.

The level of intellectual functioning for adults with Down syndrome is largely determined by ability level as a child. The benefit of early intervention programs in children with Down syndrome remains controversial but some researchers would argue that such programs can have a significant impact on the improvement of both intellectual and social skills. The possible benefits of nutritional supplementation on early intellectual and social development are discussed in chapter 2.

There is considerable variation in levels of intellectual functioning among adults with Down syndrome. There are also differences in performance for different areas of intellectual functioning eg in reading, speech and number work. In the past, the average IQ levels for adults with Down syndrome were reported to be around 30–45, the lower end of so-called 'moderate impairment'. This level is no longer accurate. It is almost certain that with better access to education and family support, many adults with Down syndrome will in the future score in the mild learning disability range and some even in the 'normal' range. Despite the fact that in adults the level of intellectual functioning is less liable to change than in children, individuals of all ages have the potential to learn new things. With appropriate input and support it is possible for many individuals with Down syndrome to perform at a relatively high level and to attain considerable achievements.

Social competence

Social competence is a general term used to describe an individual's ability with respect to degree of independence, level of self-care, ability to be responsible and interact appropriately with others. Most adults with Down syndrome can dress and undress themselves but some need support or prompting. At age 21 years approximately two-thirds of adults with Down syndrome are fully independent in toileting (day and night), and half in bathing and dressing. Nearly all adults with Down syndrome have good mobility with the vast majority able to participate in a number of sports. However, some of the characteristics associated with Down syndrome, such as obesity or heart disease, can limit an individual's capacity to enjoy some sports activities.

Adults with Down syndrome can acquire the usual self-care and personal skills but may do so at a slower pace than other adults. A small minority with severe learning disability may require significant support. Adults with Down syndrome have, until recently, had minimal support to develop a high level of social competence. However, social competence continues to improve with increasing age from adolescence into early adulthood. After this age there is a plateau effect up to the age of 40–50 years when middle-aged adults

Figure 1: Level of social competence at different ages

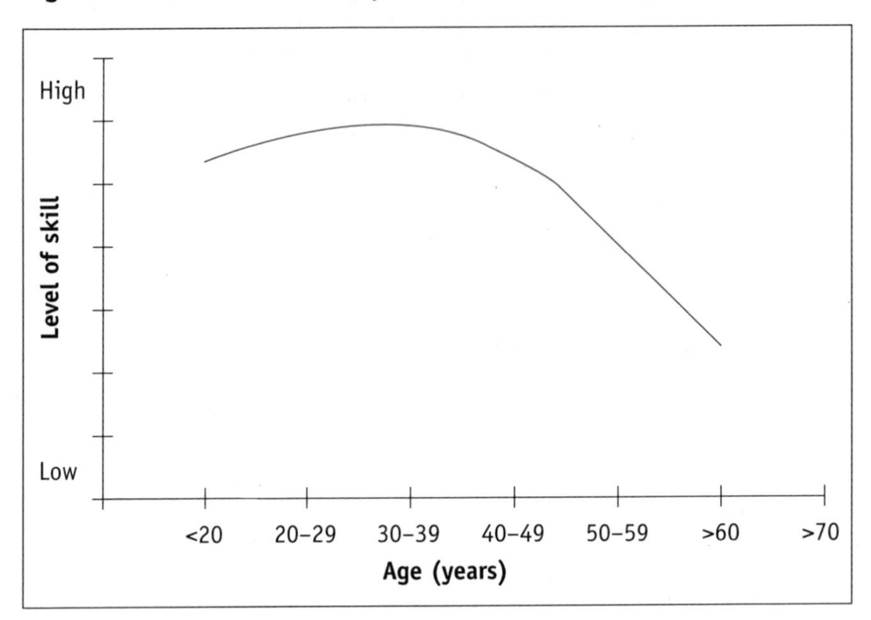

can begin to lose skills eg in mobility, toileting skills, eating and dressing/grooming. This may reflect 'premature ageing' or decline associated with the onset of dementia (chapter 16).

It is important to bear in mind that a high proportion of older adults with Down syndrome do not suffer from any significant physical and medical problems which can affect maintenance of self-care and independence skills. Most older adults are quite able in terms of feeding, bathing, toileting and dressing. If appropriate consideration is given to the healthcare needs of people with Down syndrome the opportunities for self-development and growth in terms of both intellectual and self-care skills will be greatly improved.

Chapter 2

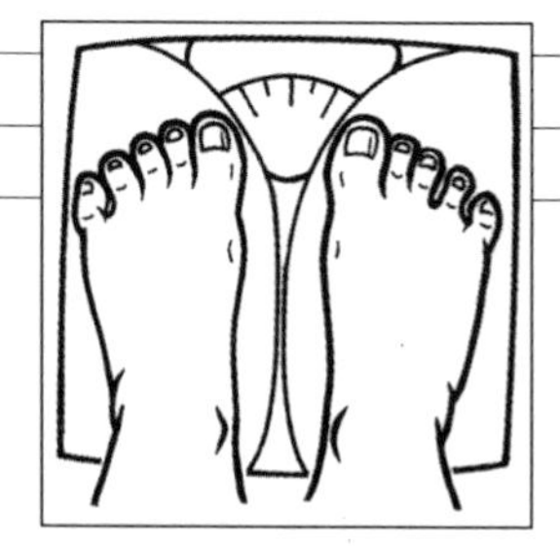

GROWTH AND NUTRITION

Growth and nutrition relate to the use of food for optimum physical and mental growth. A good diet requires a balance of proteins, carbohydrates, fats, vitamins, minerals, fibre and water. Such essentials are obtained from a wide variety of food which includes milk and milk products, vegetables, fruits, bread, cereals, meat and eggs. For people with Down syndrome, physical and mental growth has been shown to be delayed. Inadequate nutritional status may prove to be a significant factor causing this.

Stature

Adults with Down syndrome are generally shorter compared to the general population. The life-span curve for the average age-related height for adults with Down syndrome is similar in shape to that for the general population but, as expected, is significantly lower at all ages (Figure 2). Men with Down syndrome are taller than women with Down syndrome of the same age, by, on average, 7 centimetres. The peak in height appears to occur around late twenties to mid-thirties of age, some 5–10 years later than that for the general population. Similar to the general population, after middle-age, there is a slow reduction in height with increasing age. The height of an adult with Down syndrome must be compared to other adults with Down syndrome of the same sex and age and not with that for the general adult population before unnecessary anxiety is raised regarding the short stature. Growth hormone therapy has been given

Figure 2: Average height distribution for Down syndrome and general population

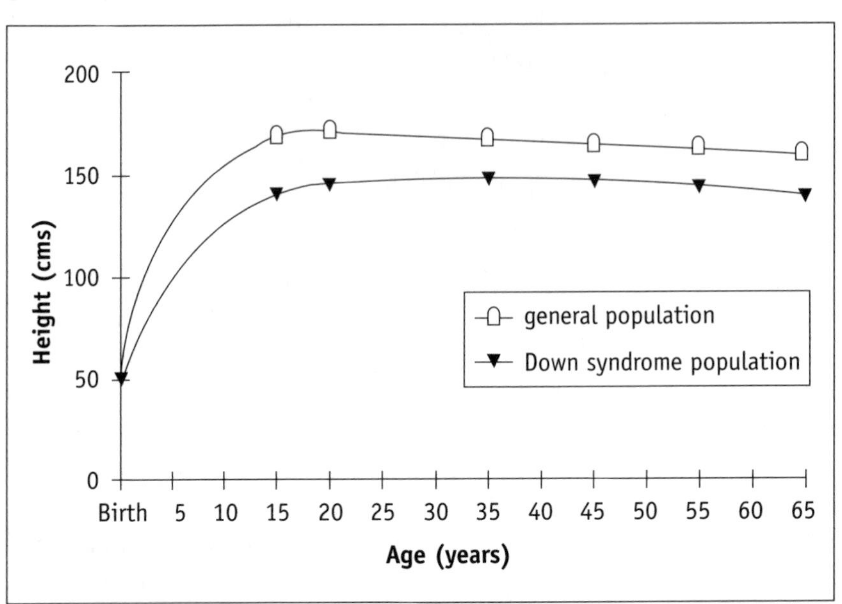

to children with Down syndrome to improve their height. However, such therapy remains controversial and is of no proven benefit in adults (chapter 15).

Obesity

Obesity is an increase in body weight beyond that which is necessary for one's height, as a result of excess body fat. It is a more severe form of being overweight. A standard way of measuring obesity is to use 'body mass index' (BMI). This is the weight in kilograms divided by the square of the height in metres (weight in kg/height in metres^2). The different levels of obesity are given in Table 2.

Obesity is a common problem for the general population and more so for people with Down syndrome (Figure 3). In the general population 34% of adult males and 24% of adult females are said to be overweight (BMI 25–29). Six per cent of males and 8% of

Table 2: Body Mass Index (BMI)*

Underweight	less than 21
Desirable weight	21–24
Overweight	25–29
Obese	30–34
Medically significant obesity	35–39
Super-obesity	40–44
Morbid obesity	more than 44

females are reported to be obese (BMI greater than 30). Among the Down syndrome adult population only 12% have 'desirable weight' (BMI 21-24), 29% have been shown to be 'overweight' (BMI 25–29) and a further 48% 'obese' (BMI greater than 30). Twenty-five per cent have levels of obesity at or above the 'medically significant' level (BMI greater than 35). For adults with Down syndrome being overweight or obese is a major problem at all ages, but in particular for younger adults.

Why people become obese remains unclear but there is an imbalance of excess energy intake to energy loss. Obese people do not necessarily eat more than required. Generally for people with Down syndrome a number of factors are important: excessive calorie intake, low metabolic rate with burning of less energy, less physical activity (associated with decreased muscle tone, delayed development, reduced physical activity), side-effects of medication and hormonal abnormalities (eg hypothyroidism). Heredity factors, emotional problems and the cultural setting are other important factors. Obesity often begins in early childhood with adult obesity reflecting childhood obesity.

For any adult with Down syndrome who is suspected of being overweight or obese, the weight and if possible the calorie intake

Figure 3: Distribution of average body mass by age and sex

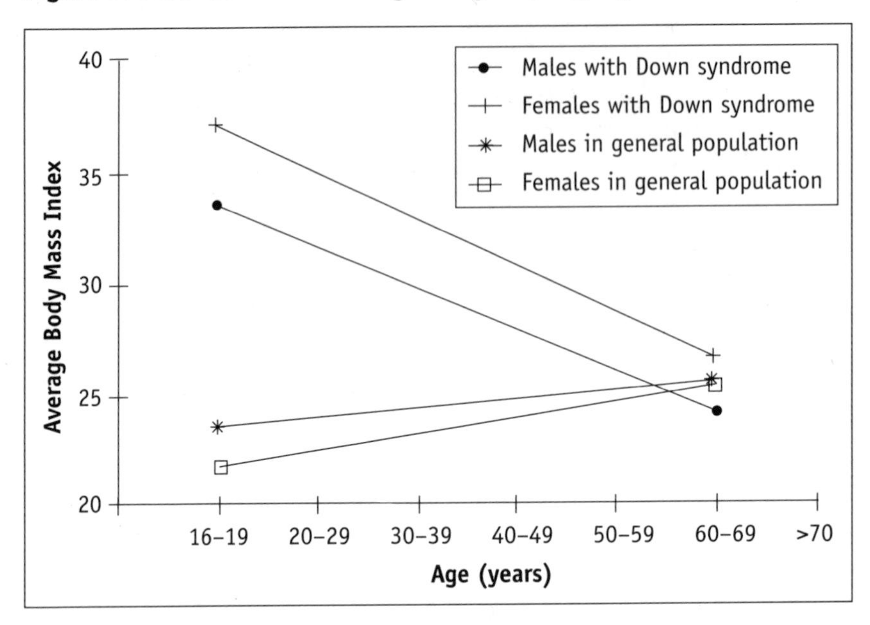

should be measured on a regular basis. An excessive increase in weight over a short period of time for no apparent reason should be investigated eg for hypothyroidism. In common with the general population people with Down syndrome are susceptible to other complications associated with obesity. These include lung disease, arthritis (hands, knees, spine, hips), diabetes, heart disease, hypertension, strokes, thyroid dysfunction and digestive problems. It is important that people receive appropriate support and health care for these complications. (Appendix I).

There are now a number of popular magazines and books on dieting and how best to lose weight. The principles given generally apply also to adults with Down syndrome: the need for a change in diet, change in behaviour with respect to food and support from others. It may be helpful for individuals to have the advice and support of a dietician. The only way to really lose weight is by a reduction in calorie intake eg to 1000kcal/day and to increase exercise (especially aerobics which increases metabolic rate). Self help groups and behavioural programmes recommended by health professionals can reinforce and help to maintain motivation. Drug therapies are available which can reduce appetite but these are not recommended by doctors. Surgery, for example wiring of the jaws, removal of a part of the stomach to make the person feel 'full' quickly and reduction of the digestive system to reduce food absorption have been tried in the general population but should not be performed on people with Down syndrome without expert medical advice. One problem is that dramatic weight loss will usually lead to weight loss being regained when normal dieting resumes. Better education of individuals and carers to prevent obesity in the first place and improved access to health promotion can prevent future problems (chapter 3).

Nutrition

People with Down syndrome may have lower blood levels of some substances than the general population (for example calcium), have impaired glucose metabolism or lower levels of some bodily enzymes. It remains important to compare findings for any one person with Down syndrome to those for the Down syndrome population. A low measure may be normal for a person with Down syndrome. Wasted time and considerable distress can be caused by fruitless investigations looking for a reason when something is found to be apparently 'abnormal'. **Medical advice from a specialist who cares for adults with Down syndrome should be sought if there are any concerns regarding nutritional deficiency or if abnormalities are found on routine tests. Certainly if there are other associated symptoms or signs then an expert opinion should be sought.**

A deficiency of carbohydrates and/or proteins is unlikely to occur in Western countries. However it may occur where there is a restriction of diet, for example due to food fads or a loss of interest in food following a medical illness. The older anticonvulsant drugs (eg Phenytoin, Phenobarbitone) used to control epilepsy, can lead to folate deficiency. Maintaining a good diet should prevent nutritional deficiency. If present, replacement therapy may be required.

Nutritional excess will occur if the calorie intake is greater than the amount of calories used up. This may lead to the development of obesity (above). Excessive intake of minerals and/or vitamins can lead to nutritional disorders eg excessive salt intake can cause hypertension, excessive vitamin intake can cause nerve damage.

Vitamins and targeted nutritional intervention (specially formulated combinations of vitamins, minerals, hormones, enzymes, and amino acid supplements)

Megavitamin therapy to improve the intelligence, speech, height and health of children with Down syndrome has been previously advocated but research has generally failed to confirm these claims. Some studies have reported benefit from vitamin supplementation on immune function with a possible greater resistance to infections. The role of selenium (a mineral) and vitamin E in reducing effects of ageing are being investigated at present but further research is still required. At present no nutritional substance can definitely be advocated to improve intelligence or general health in people with Down syndrome. **A specialist medical opinion is advisable.**

Chapter 3

A HEALTHY LIFESTYLE

A healthy lifestyle is determined by a person's constitution and by the way he or she lives their life. A positive approach to a healthy lifestyle can enhance the quality of an individual's life, prevent or reduce the risk of illness and early death and minimise the need for medical help.

Healthy Eating

Food is essential for survival as it gives the body the energy needed for growth and for leading an active life. Healthy eating enables people to access a better quality of life by reducing the risk of serious physical and psychological problems. There are also many social benefits of being fit and well and feeling good.

Overweight and obesity is probably the most obvious outcome of unhealthy eating (chapter 2). A balanced diet is the best means of keeping weight in proportion to one's height. We are all familiar with what foods are supposed to constitute a healthy diet and what foods we should avoid, or at least go carefully on. The guidelines for a healthy diet are:

- eat a variety of foods
- eat plenty of foods rich in starch and fibre, such as wholemeal bread, potatoes, pasta, cereals
- eat fruit or vegetables each day

- maintain a diet containing a balance of vitamins, minerals and pure water
- don't eat too much fat or too many sugary things
- keep within the recommended limits for alcohol
- **above all, enjoy your food!**

Keeping to a 'healthy weight' is sometimes difficult. It's not so easy, especially as one grows older. Chocolate and ice-creams and so on are delicious and often form part of a social outing. Going to the pub can be very enjoyable and it's hard to resist an extra pint. If extra advice and help is required it is possible to contact a State Registered Dietician. Dieticians may be contacted through your GP's practice or by referral to a hospital or NHS Community Trust. Keeping to a sensible weight has many advantages and it's better to tackle the issue sooner than later. People with Down syndrome have a tendency to suffer from hypothyroidism which can lead to putting on extra weight, so regular health checks are a must.

Recreation and Exercise

Regular exercise is just as important as healthy eating for a healthy lifestyle. Exercise maintains good health and reduces premature ageing.

Most adults with Down syndrome will be able to walk, run, swim and take part in many physical activities. While still at school children with Down syndrome should be encouraged to take part in physical education and sports and out-door activities. Even people who have severe physical disabilities are able to participate in some sporting activities and derive a great deal of enjoyment and benefit from them. Such benefit can include better mobility, opportunity to make relationships and better health.

People with Down syndrome are at risk from atlanto-axial instability (weakness found in the upper part of the spine – see chapter 13). There are many 'safe' sporting and physical activities such as running, swimming, walking and dancing. Decisions about the suitability of other sports and activities must be taken on an individual basis with the advice of a professional such as a physiotherapist.

As young people gain greater independence, leave school and have more control over their social life, they may experience difficulties in establishing a social life which includes physical activity. This is particularly so if they require high levels of support to access community facilities which are available. With careful planning and support, people with Down syndrome can access and enjoy the full range of social and leisure activities available in their community.

Local leisure centres, social clubs and community centres are all useful links which may be explored, as are colleges of further education which often offer specialist evening classes for people with learning disabilities.

Exercise may take the form of different activities but generally is based on the following principles:

- activity is greater during exercise than activity engaged in at home, day placement, or at work
- exercise activity continues for 20–30 minutes three times a week
- warm-up and cool-down sessions are important
- no abnormal strain is involved
- exercise is incorporated into the weekly routine
- **exercise is enjoyable!**

Support and encouragement is often needed to enable individuals to fully engage in community activities. Support may be forthcoming from others: your GP, health visitor, school nurse, dietician, doctor, dentist or sports centre. Or try contacting support organisations: The British Sports Association for the Disabled, United Kingdom Sports Association for People with Learning Disability, MENCAP, PHAB (Physically Handicapped and Able Bodied), Riding for the Disabled (Appendix C). All provide sports and leisure services, facilities or information for members of these organisations who have a disability.

Screening of medical problems (Appendix A) is an important aspect of a healthy lifestyle and must go hand-in-hand with healthy eating and exercise. **The aim of leading a healthy life is to keep well and enjoy life to the full.**

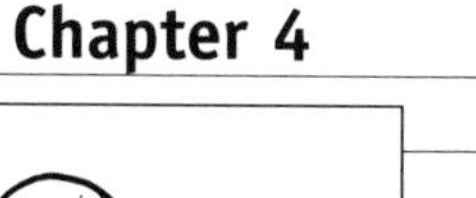

Chapter 4

SEXUALITY, SEX EDUCATION AND SEXUAL HEALTH

For all of us, growing and developing into responsible adults also includes enjoying positive friendships and relationships which include the full range of emotional experience, and may include sexual expression.

This is equally important for people with Down syndrome. It is important that the feelings of individuals are valued and people are enabled to express themselves appropriately.

Sexuality

Sometimes it is difficult for parents to accept the sexual feelings and needs of their adolescent sons and daughters. Parents and carers of people with a learning disability may find it even more difficult. They may have fears about the vulnerability of the person with a learning disability, about possible unacceptable sexual behaviour, even about what other people will say or think about it all. It can be easier to hold on to the idea that an adult with a learning disability will remain a 'child' or 'child-like' throughout life – being dependent, needing protection and not needing to express themselves sexually.

People with Down syndrome experience the same range of emotions and feelings as the general population and enjoy the positive friendships and relationships that the rest of us do. These may include the full range of sexual expression as well as sexuality: people will be heterosexual, gay, may wish to marry, or may choose to live with a partner. People may experience sexual expression within these relationships or choose not to. However, all positive relationships provide love, support and increased self-esteem. It is also possible that masturbation may be the only form of sexual expression for some people.

All aspects of sexual expression and relationship building will form an important part of an individual's education as they develop into adults.

Sex education

Parents of a son or daughter with Down syndrome who received sex education at school were probably helped to understand more about his or her developmental needs and ways in which these might be met. They may have been involved in discussion with teachers over the content and method of 'sex education'. Sex education in schools is part of Health Education that also covers family life education, safety and personal hygiene and education for citizenship. In this way, sex education is put into context as part of a programme that aims to develop knowledge and understanding that enables young people to function at a more mature level, physically, emotionally and socially.

Some people with Down syndrome may not have had much, if indeed any, sex education. It is only fairly recently that it has been given the attention it deserves, especially in special schools, where it may have been thought 'not necessary'. It is also important to remember that 'education' is not something we get at school and then cease to need. We all go on adding to our stock of knowledge and understanding throughout life. We learn through talking and listening to other people, reading, observing, through the media and through social opportunities. Some or all of these types of opportunities for learning may not be available to people with Down syndrome. We cannot rely on them continuing to learn and develop unless given opportunities that are appropriate for them.

Sex education may continue in colleges or training centres but many adults with Down syndrome may not be supported in this way. Leaving them in ignorance is not really an option for many reasons. In the first place, denying the sexuality of people with a learning disability is treating them in a disrespectful manner and depriving them of a valuable human experience. Secondly, for their own safety and well-being, people with a learning disability need to have basic information and achieve certain skills. Knowledge of contraception and skills to put it into practice may be required, also understanding of sexually transmitted disease such as HIV/Aids. Unfortunately, people with a learning disability are more likely to suffer sexual abuse than people in the population at large. For their own safety they need to know what is acceptable behaviour, what is not, and their right to say 'No' to behaviour that they do not wish to permit. Protecting themselves involves understanding their own feelings and the way their bodies work, as well as learning how to stay safe and be assertive.

Continuing advice and support on these matters may also be helpful for families and carers of people with Down syndrome. Attitudes towards the sexuality of people with Down syndrome may vary enormously, examples of two extremes being "people with Down syndrome don't do that sort of thing" and "all people with Down syndrome should be encouraged to participate in sexual intercourse". Parental and family concerns regarding possible sexual abuse are real and should be taken seriously. Appropriate counselling and education remain essential, with parent and family involvement. Special advice may not be readily available; parents and families may need to be active in seeking help. A useful book (*Sexuality and People with Intellectual Disability*) which covers a wide range of issues pertaining to sexuality and people with a learning disability is by Fegan and colleagues and was published in 1993 (Appendix B).

Consent issues

Consent to sexual activity requires that a person understands the implications of the situation, understands what is involved, understands the problems that can arise and that they should be allowed to make the decision without coercion. The number of adults with Down syndrome entering into marriage and partnerships, for whom these conditions are important, is increasing. Many are capable of making decisions about their own life but again appropriate counselling and education are required. Some people may need support to explore the issues. Section 7 of the Sexual Offence Act 1956 states that is an offence to have sexual intercourse with a person with a severe learning disability, outside marriage. For further information on the Law and its implications see Fegan et al (1993) (see Appendix B for details).

Reproduction issues

Women with Down syndrome can be fertile, may get pregnant and subsequently give birth. With the appropriate level of support, people with a learning disability can care for a baby adequately. Although the above outcomes are extremely uncommon, professionals and carers must be aware of the possibilities. If a woman with Down syndrome does become pregnant there is an increased likelihood that the offspring will have Down syndrome. Recently it was reported that of 30 pregnancies in women with Down syndrome (where the father did not have Down syndrome) 10 babies were born with Down syndrome and the others with no birth problem. Due to the small stature of women with Down syndrome, vaginal birth delivery may not be possible and the need for a Caesarean section increases. The presence of other problems such as diabetes, epilepsy and thyroid disease can all affect pregnancy and peri-natal care. Obviously, issues relating to pregnancy should be discussed with both partners so that they can choose what is right for them and make plans accordingly.

Many males with Down syndrome are relatively infertile due to a low sperm count or reduced motility of sperm which makes procreation unlikely but not impossible – for example, in 1990, for the first time a man with Down syndrome became a father.

Contraception

For many people the oral contraceptive pill remains the first choice. Benefits of the pill include reduced dysmenorrhoea (period pain), reduced infection and reduced risk of ovarian cancer. However, side-effects such as nausea, headache, thrombosis and hypertension can occur and a history of seizures, liver disease, cardiovascular disease may all prevent the use of the pill. Important interactions with other drugs such as anti-convulsants (group of drugs used to treat epilepsy, for example carbamazepine, sodium valproate, phenytoin) can also occur.

Intrauterine devices are of limited use in people with a learning disability. Increased dysmenorrhoea and infections can be quite serious in people with reduced awareness of possible symptoms. Insertion and regular checkups may also be upsetting for a person with a learning disability.

Depo-Provera, a long-acting form of the contraceptive pill injected into the muscle, is available. It is an injection of the hormone progestogen given once every three months. It is reliable and there are no proven side-effects apart from those similar to the oral contraceptive pill (above). It can be used as an alternative for women for whom an oestrogen containing pill is contraindicated.

Barrier methods (condoms, diaphragms) can be of value but require consistent attention to practice and a degree of self-discipline that may be difficult for many people with a learning disability. Training and practice for both partners is necessary.

Sterilisation

Carer concern about young women with Down syndrome becoming pregnant remains high, with parents not uncommonly asking about sterilisation. Although often the choice of parents of young people with Down syndrome, sterilisation (tubal ligation for women, vasectomy for men) remains controversial. If a person with Down syndrome understands all aspects of the procedure and can give informed consent the procedure may be carried out. Informed consent means that they must understand that the procedure involves an operation with the result that they will never be able to have children. If informed consent is not possible then, in the UK, legal action through the Court has to be undertaken.

Sexual health

It is important that people with a learning disability are as able to benefit from the same preventative measures as everyone else. Regular check-ups are an essential part of maintaining good sexual health in order that treatment may be carried out if necessary. Coupled with education in the reasons for such check-ups, the person with a learning disability should be helped to understand the risks to health that are posed by such agents as smoking and unprotected sex.

Breast checks in the form of breast examination once a month are important as the first step in detecting problems. Some women with Down syndrome will be able to carry out the check-ups by themselves; others may need help from carers and yearly examinations by a doctor. All women with Down syndrome should also be enabled to participate in breast screening programmes at the same intervals as the general population. An illustrated guide *Keep Yourself Healthy: A Guide to Checking your Breasts* designed for use by girls and women with learning difficulties, is available from the Family Advice and Information Resource Centre (Appendix B). Other helpful illustrated books are *Looking after my Breasts* and

Good Practice in Breast and Cervical Screening for Women with Learning Disabilities to promote good practice. (Appendix B).

Cervical smear tests likewise aim to detect changes that may become cancerous so that early treatment may be carried out. Preparation is necessary to ensure that the woman understands what is involved in a pelvic examination. (See the publication '*Good Practice in Breast and Cervical Screening for Women with Learning Disabilities*') for further information (Appendix 2). *Keeping Healthy Down Below* explains and illustrates the examination for women with learning disabilities.

As with breast checks by women, some men will be able to examine their own testicles; others will need to be examined by a doctor or a specialist nurse. Men with Down syndrome are reported to have an increased risk of testicular cancer. Therefore, regular examination is important.

Sexually transmitted diseases

While gonorrhoea and syphilis are easily treatable if the symptoms are recognised, symptoms of some other sexually transmitted diseases are not so obvious. A person infected with HIV virus can, at the moment, only receive treatment that slows down the progress of the disease.

It is therefore vitally important that people with a learning disability are helped to understand the means and risk of catching a sexually transmitted disease and the ways in which such risks may be avoided or reduced – use of condoms, maintaining a monogamous relationship, or not having sexual intercourse.

Chapter 5

HEALTH PROFESSIONALS AND SERVICES OF SUPPORT

Health professionals

People with Down syndrome are entitled to the same standard of healthcare as everyone else. Unfortunately, not all healthcare professionals are knowledgeable about their general and particular health needs. The onus of obtaining appropriate attention and care sometimes falls on the person's family or carers, especially if the person with Down syndrome has difficulty describing the source of pain or discomfort. In this case it can be helpful to have a good knowledge of what various professionals can offer and where to go for help. Many carers will have learned this from experience but the following list may be of help to others.

1. The General Practitioner (GP)
For the majority of people with Down syndrome who live in the community, the main provider of healthcare is their general practitioner (GP), along with other professionals who together make up the primary health care team. GPs are easily accessible (or should be so). Usually the GP knows the family and may know the person with Down syndrome – they may have always looked after him or her.

As was explained in the introduction of this book, adults with Down syndrome are more likely than other people to suffer from a range of illnesses and medical conditions that require treatment. Particular physical disorders include sensory impairment, overweight and obesity, and thyroid dysfunction. Particular psychiatric disorders include dementia, depression and obsessive-compulsive disorders. This does not mean that all adults with Down syndrome will develop these disorders but it does mean that health services should be aware of their diagnosis, treatment and management. Some people with Down syndrome find it difficult to communicate any pain or discomfort associated with a given illness. If ill health is missed or misdiagnosed, much suffering may be caused which could have been avoided. For these reasons, people with Down syndrome should receive regular health checks and this has been recommended by the Royal College of General Practitioners. Appendix A gives the important aspects of health which should be checked on a regular basis.

Resources which might be useful

(i) Some people with Down syndrome may be worried about going to the doctors. Some may be uncooperative, causing anxiety to carers and most importantly, lessening the likelihood that they will receive proper care and attention. Understanding and skill on the part of healthcare professionals can go a long way to reducing fears but so can good preparation and support on the part of carers. There are some useful illustrative books that familiarise the patient with what will happen. Some are suitable for children and some for adults. An example of the latter is *Going to the Doctor* published by St George's Mental Health Library (see Appendix B for details). This book can be used by supporters alongside the person with a learning disability. It is also a useful resource for GPs and the primary care team. It emphasises the issue of consent and provides pictures that help to clarify the patient's choices. Many organisations for people with learning disabilities have produced booklets that describe what happens when receiving treatments, by means of signs, symbols and drawings. Some booklets have been produced by people with a learning disability who understand the needs of others.

(ii) If families or carers are not certain of rights in respect to healthcare, it may be helpful to consult *The Patient's Charter and You*. This can be obtained from The Patient's Charter and You, Tel 0870 1555455, Department of Health, PO Box 777, London SE99

7XU. It is produced in different languages, on audio cassette, in Braille, large print, on video and in British Sign Language. Most importantly there is a version with signs and symbols for people with learning disabilities. Specify the version(s) you require when ordering.

(iii) Information about health services in your area may be obtained by calling your local health authority. The *Health Information Service* (0845 4647) will give information on health services and health-related subjects. Calls are free and confidential.

Many GP practices are supported by a team of other healthcare professionals (a primary health care team) and it is becoming increasingly common to find that a range of services is offered at health centres. If this is the situation in your area, it can be very helpful to have the services of nurses, health visitors, physiotherapists, chiropodists, social workers and a pharmacy service all under one roof. Travelling around in order to obtain different services can be costly, time-consuming and tiring but, as yet, by no means everyone has access to a 'supermarket' type of primary healthcare. It is useful to know which professionals provide which service.

2. Paediatricians

Paediatricians are doctors who specialise principally in child health but may also see young adults with Down syndrome. They assess, diagnose and care for children, from young babies through to older teenagers with medical and developmental problems. Multi-professional community paediatric services are responsible for monitoring the development of children and young adults with learning difficulties. The paediatrician works in conjunction with health visitors, school nurses, speech and language therapists, occupational therapists and physiotherapists. Paediatricians can arrange for the appropriate transfer of medical care of a young adult with Down syndrome from child services to adult services. Such transfers should be initiated and discussed at least one year before implementation. This gives time to allow the necessary adult educational, social and medical needs to be met.

3. Psychiatrists

Psychiatrists in learning disability have particular expertise in the physical and mental problems associated with learning disability. Since adults with Down syndrome are at greater risk than the general population of developing an emotional or psychological disorder (see Chapter 16) it is important to obtain specialist advice on diagnosis, cause, assessment, appropriate treatment and outlook. Many psychiatrists do undertake routine health screening, although this is often undertaken by GPs.

4. The Community Learning Disability Team (CLDT)

These teams have been set up to serve the particular needs of people with a learning disability and their carers. Some teams are very small while others contain several professionals such as a psychiatrist, psychologist, occupational therapist, speech and language therapist, in addition to community nurses and social workers. Professionals in the team will understand the particular health and social problems of people with a learning disability and can provide valuable support. Regular meetings are held by the team to discuss in a multi-professional forum the needs of each person with a learning disability in contact with the services.

5. Community nurses

Community nurses in learning disability (CNLDs) can give support and advice to adults with Down syndrome and their carers in their home. If necessary, a nurse from the community learning disability team will accompany the person with Down syndrome to the GP surgery to explain about particular health needs and problems. Community nurses can help with aspects such as supervision of medication, responding to mental health and epilepsy needs, knowledge of day services, obesity, incontinence and help to create packages of care. Community nurses and other members of the team can put you in touch with other services, if required.

6. Social workers/care managers

Although social workers are not directly concerned with healthcare, attention to the social well-being of the person with Down syndrome and his or her carers is essential for a satisfactory and satisfying life style.

If not based in the CLDT, social workers with expertise in learning disability may be based in social services teams in the community, sometimes in a local health centre or in a team attached to a hospital. They are responsible for assessing the needs of both the person with Down syndrome and of the carers and family. They will then give information on welfare benefits, services and equipment and the sources of support, recreation and training that are available locally.

7. Physiotherapists

Many physiotherapists now work in GP surgeries or health centres and visit people's homes to provide advice and treatment. Using various techniques, such as exercise, electrotherapy and acupuncture they can help with a wide range of joint problems, chest conditions, incontinence, pain or difficulties in movement and lack of balance and control of limbs.

8. Occupational therapists

The occupational therapist aims to assess the general level of function of each person in the areas of self-care, productivity or work activity and occupational skills – areas of importance to the general well-being, independence and development of a person with a learning disability. Therapists work as part of a multidisciplinary team in CLDTs or in the NHS hospital trusts and offer guidance and advice to individuals and families as well as carrying out therapeutic programmes.

9. Speech and language therapists

Speech and language therapists are trained in the assessment of communication (verbal and non-verbal), in speech and language disorders and in the application of many varied treatments to enable a person with a learning disability to function as well as possible in his or her environment. Stammering, articulation difficulties, eating and drinking, and voice disorders are only some of the problems helped by speech and language therapy. Training and supervision of care workers is also an important role of the therapist.

10. Psychologists
Psychologists work as part of a team with professionals from other disciplines to assess the intellectual strengths or weaknesses of the adult with Down sydrome and advise on their educational and psychological needs. Psychologists also have training and experience in managing behaviour, should such advice be needed.

11. Dieticians
If there are problems with overweight or obesity that are difficult to overcome, a hospital or community State Registered Dietician will assess the nutritional adequacy of a given diet and give detailed advice. Since the dangers and disadvantages of obesity have been well described, it is important that people with Down syndrome follow a healthy dietary regime that does not contribute to excess weight. The aim is to give people a consistent and practical message about healthy eating. The British Dietetic Association can provide names of dieticians, NHS and freelance, working in your area.

Services which offer support

A wide range of services is available for adults with Down syndrome. These will vary from country to country, and from region to region but many services will overlap.

1. Hearing aid services
The NHS hearing aid service is free and includes testing, fitting, servicing, and provision of batteries. If in doubt about whether or not a person with Down syndrome is hearing well, the first port of call is the GP who will probably refer to a hearing aid centre or to a hospital Ear Nose and Throat department. Professionals at hearing aid centres may not always be able to meet the needs of a person with a learning disability. In this case it can be useful to contact a hearing aid therapist with experience in this field. They are not available in all NHS areas but can provide valuable help when assessment is difficult and/or the hearing aid user has problems in

benefiting from the aid. Other people, such as nurses working in CLDTs or specialist social workers, may also have experience in helping people to get maximum benefit from a hearing aid. The Royal National Institute for the Deaf (RNID) can provide extra advice and support, if required.

2. Services for the visually impaired

Some visual impairments are very common among people with Down syndrome and it is important that advice should be sought early. Routine visits to the optometrist (person trained to examine and test eyes and prescribed correcting lenses) should be made to check on visual acuity (sharpness of vision), on the correct deviation of light by the lens of the eye, and cataracts. As with hearing problems, help and advice are available from your GP and members of the Community Learning Disability Team. A home visit from an optometrist can be arranged if necessary. Apart from spectacles, low vision aids, including hand and stand magnifiers can be prescribed through the NHS. Professional help and training may be needed to help some people with Down syndrome to make the most of restricted vision. The Royal National Institute for the Blind (RNIB) or the Partially Sighted Society provides information on mobility aids, benefits, technology, social services and education.

3. Dental Care Services

While there are community dentists who are able to meet the special needs of people with Down syndrome, many carers report difficulty in finding one locally. At present there is very little financial incentive for family dentists to give the additional time or effort that might be required. Many areas have at least one senior dentist with experience of providing dental care for people with a learning disability but this service is not always well publicised. A computer-assisted learning pack for dental practitioners *Dentistry for Special Needs* has been funded by the Department of Health (Bedi and Pollard, 1995) – see Appendix B for further details. You may wish to tell your dentist about it.

4. Respite care services

These offer a temporary opportunity for adults with Down syndrome to spend time away from their parents and families. This enables the family to 'have a break' and can enable the person with Down syndrome to be more independent. They are usually managed and paid for by Social or Health services. Respite care services vary from district to district, some are better served than others.

5. Down syndrome organisations

These have usually been formed by parents of children with Down syndrome and are able to provide a wide range of support through newsletters, meetings, literature and funding of research (see Appendix C for details).

6. Voluntary organisations

There are many organisations which can provide help for people with a disability. The booklet *A Practical Guide for Disabled People: Where to find information, services and equipment* – Appendix B, lists the names, addresses and phone numbers of many such organisations. It also suggests that if the one you are looking for is not listed, it may be helpful to try the *Directory for Disabled People*, your local public library or information centre, your local DIAL or Disabled Living Centre or the Health Information Service.

7. The internet

A rapidly growing source of information to those who have a computer is the 'World Wide Web'. Information includes that from people with Down syndrome talking about themselves, information from organisations and from Research Centres. Parents and/or carers may also find it useful to communicate with other parents and carers of people with Down syndrome (See Appendix C for Internet sites).

SPECIFIC MEDICAL ISSUES

Chapter 6

VISION AND RELATED PROBLEMS

The shape of the eyes is often the first indication that a new-born baby may have Down syndrome and historically the appearance of the eyes was influential in the adoption of the term 'mongolism'. Many abnormalities of the eye (Figure 4) occur, with the most common due to errors of focusing (short-sightedness, long-sightedness). Some features of the eyes cause no significant problems (for example upward slanting eyes or speckling of the iris) whilst others can impair vision significantly (for example cataracts and glaucoma). Many of the eye problems increase with age and may remain undetected for some time leading to significant physical, mental, educational and social difficulties. It is important, therefore, for regular screening for visual and related problems to be undertaken. The earlier a problem is identified the better the outlook after treatment. **If concerned a doctor's opinion should always be sought.** An assessment by an ophthalmologist or specialist may be required.

Short-sightedness (myopia):

Cause: The focusing power of the eyes is too strong leading to light rays being brought to a focus in front of the retina (back of the eye) rather than as should happen on the retina.

Symptoms and signs: Difficulty in seeing is often not reported by individuals or detected by carers. Close objects are still seen clearly but objects further away are blurred and not in focus. Symptoms can include eyestrain, headaches, deterioration in day-to-day activities or deterioration in behaviour.

Figure 4: The different parts of an eye

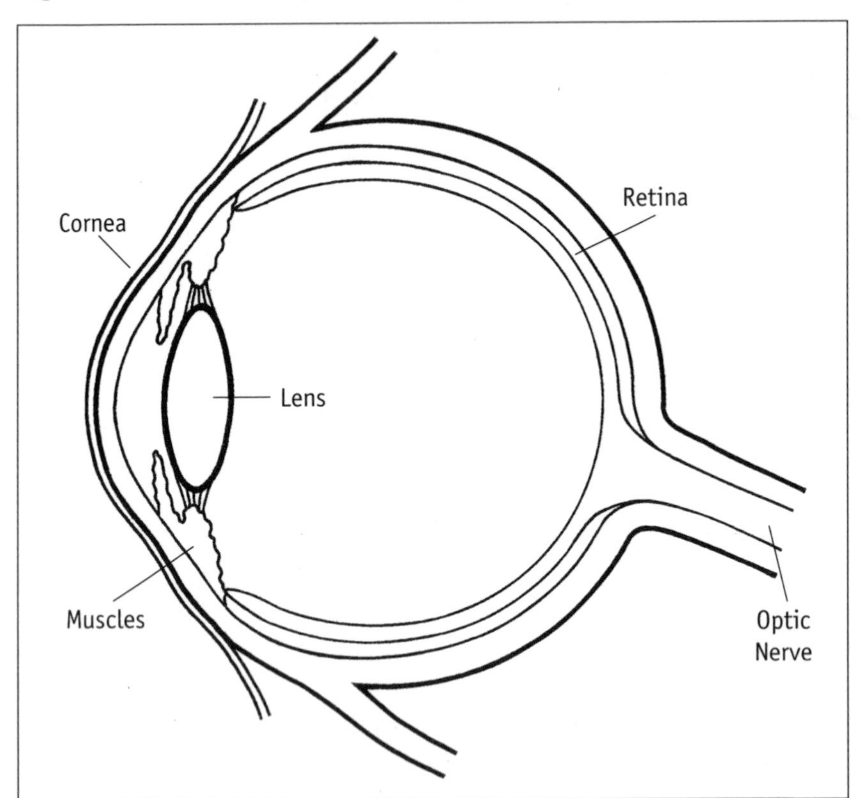

Investigations: The assessment of vision by an optometrist (person trained to examine and test eyes and prescribed correcting lenses) or by the hospital Eye Department is required if loss in vision is suspected. Time and patience is required for a successful assessment.

Complications: Usually none but occasionally can lead to an increase in accidents or mis-diagnosis of deterioration in behaviour as caused by an emotional problem (depression or dementia).

Treatment and Prevention: The prescribing of glasses or contact lenses is now standard. Fitting and getting the person to wear them can, however, be difficult. Breakage or loss is common and it is recommended that a spare set is readily available. The use of visual aids and modification to the environment (eg greater use of lighting and colour) can be of considerable benefit. Regular check-ups (every 1–2 years) are recommended.

Long-sightedness (hypermetropia):

Cause: The focusing power of the eyes is too weak. Light rays are brought to a focus behind the retina and not on it.

Symptoms and signs: Similar to short-sightedness, problems may not be reported by individuals or detected by carers. Usually there is difficulty in seeing close objects in focus although far vision can also be affected. Occasionally eyestrain and headaches can occur.

Investigations: See short-sightedness (above).

Complications: Usually none but there is an increased risk of glaucoma developing (below).

Treatment and prevention: See short-sightedness (above).

Astigmatism: A condition of the eye where the surface of the cornea is not smoothly 'spherical'.

Causes: Often the cause is unknown. Can be present at birth or can occur because of other eye problems eg keratoconus (below).

Symptoms and signs: Difficulty in seeing may not be reported by individuals or detected by carers. Can include blurring of vision, eyestrain and headaches.

Investigations/Complications/Treatment: See short-sightedness (above). A particular form of glasses is required.

Accommodation (Abnormal): The inability of the eye to change focus correctly such that both near and far objects can be seen clearly and in focus.

Causes: Due to the impairment in the elasticity of the eye lens and impairment in the action of the muscles of the eye. Can be present in newborn babies with Down syndrome.

Symptoms and signs: Usually difficulty in focusing on close objects.

Investigations/Complications/Treatment: See short-sightedness (above).

Squint (Strabismus): The deviation of one eye from the other eye. Extremely common. Can lead to the brain receiving two images and ignoring image from one eye ('lazy eye').

Causes: Unknown but often present at birth. Rarely due to an underlying eye or brain disorder.

Symptoms and signs: Usually the eye(s) turn in. Occasionally the eye(s) turn out.

Investigations: Detect by 'corneal reflection' where reflection from a bright light falls symmetrically on each cornea if no squint, asymmetrically if squint present. Further investigations usually not required unless a squint occurs when previously not present. May need to then investigate for an underlying problem (eg nerve palsy). Should be detected as part of a health screening assessment.

Complications: Can lead to a deterioration in vision in the 'lazy eye'.

Treatment: Usually none. Glasses can be prescribed to reduce the squint. Surgical correction is possible.

Inflammation of the eyelids (blepharitis): A common condition.

Causes: Usually due to a bacterial infection. The risk of an infection is increased due to a blockage of the duct draining tears, to dry eyes and skin disease in adults with Down syndrome.

Symptoms and signs: Usually there is a red eyelid margin, irritable eyelids, a burning sensation in the eye and dry flakes on eyelid.

Investigations: Usually none required as the diagnosis can be made just by observation.

Complications: Rubbing of the eyes can lead to the eyelid turning out or turning in. Ingrowing eyelashes can occur or in a few cases, conjunctivitis (below) can also develop.

Treatment and prevention: The eyelids need to be kept clean. Any crusts present should be removed with warm water or cotton wool swabs dipped in a dilute solution of sodium bicarbonate or in baby shampoo. Antibiotic ointment or weak steroids can be used. Any underlying skin, dry eyes or scalp problem that is present will also require treatment.

Conjunctivitis: An inflammation of the membrane covering the eye.

Causes: Usually due to a bacterial or viral infection. Other causes can include an allergy (increased sensitivity to a substance), something in the eye and excessive wearing of contact lenses.

Symptoms and signs: The commonest symptom is a red eye. Other symptoms include a weeping eye, an uncomfortable feeling, a sticky eye, itching and blurring of vision.

Investigations: None required.

Complications: If untreated and due to an infection, the infection can spread to the other eye.

Treatment and prevention: Need to avoid rubbing of the eye as this will lead to the infection spreading. Usually conjunctivitis requires treatment with antibiotic drops (eg Chloramphenicol eye drops). If it is due to a foreign body, remove the offending particle. If it reoccurs and the person wears contact lenses then it may be necessary to change the type of contact lenses.

Cataracts: An opacity of the clear focussing lens of the eye. Can be one or both eyes.

Causes: Can be present at birth. There is an increase in risk with increasing age due to changes in the protein in the lens of the eye. Occasionally can be due to the presence of glaucoma (below) or diabetes (chapter 15).

Symptoms and signs: Gradual loss of vision, 'cloudy' lens. Not associated with pain in the eye. See short-sightedness (above).

Investigations: The presence of a grey/white pupil on examination can be seen. The assessment of any underlying impaired vision by an optometrist (person trained to examine and test eyes and prescribe correcting lenses) or by the hospital Eye Department is required.

Complications: See short-sightedness (above).

Treatment: Good-lighting. Spectacles may be of benefit when not too severe. For severe cases the lens of the eye can be removed and vision corrected with either thick spectacles, contact lenses or with an artificial lens implant.

Glaucoma: An increase in the pressure within the eye leading to impaired vision. Can be sudden or gradual.

Causes: Often no cause found. Can be associated with long-sightedness (above), diabetes (chapter 15) or trauma to the eye.

Symptoms and signs: Frequently no difficulty is experienced. Symptoms can include increased production of tears, rubbing of eyes, swelling of cornea, closure of the eye, inability to tolerate light, impaired vision and pain in the eye.

Investigations: An ophthalmologist or an eye specialist assessment is required. Need to measure the pressure within the eye and to examine eyes for further damage.

Complications: Loss of vision can occur.

Treatment: Need to reduce the pressure within the eye. This can be done by using medication (eye drops), laser treatment or by surgery.

Keratoconus: Conical protrusion of the central part of the cornea. Can affect both eyes at the same time.

Causes: Often unknown. Can occur due to excessive rubbing of the eyes.

Symptoms and signs: See short-sightedness (above).

Investigations: Severity and the effect on vision should be assessed by an ophthalmologist.

Complications: If severe and untreated permanently impaired vision can occur.

Treatment: For an acute condition need to treat the eye with eye lubricants, padding of the eye and pain relief. For a chronic condition keratoconus can be treated with glasses, contact lenses or by surgical intervention. If scarring is present a corneal transplant may be necessary.

Nystagmus: Repetitive to and fro movement usually of both eyes.

Causes: Usually present since birth. Can be due to side-effects of drugs.

Symptoms and signs: The commonest form is the constant horizontal vibrations of eyes. Nystagmus is usually not painful.

Investigations: Usually none required unless due to an underlying cause or occurs when previously not present. Should be identified as part of the health screening assessment.

Complications: The vision can be affected. Odd head postures can develop to reduce the effect of nystagmus.

Treatment: No need for medical intervention unless there is an underlying cause which requires treatment.

Chapter 7

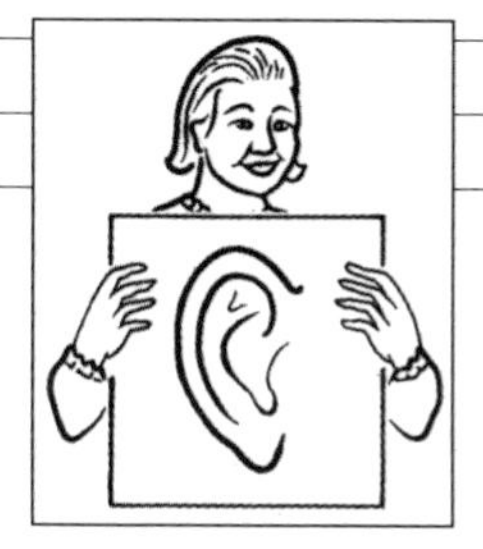

HEARING AND RELATED PROBLEMS

The ear has three parts: outer, middle and inner (Figure 5). Sound enters the outer ear and moves through the ear canal to vibrate the ear drum and small bones in the middle ear. Vibrations are then passed on to the inner ear (cochlea) and are transmitted by a nerve (auditory nerve) to the hearing centre in the brain. Problems can

Figure 5: Parts of the ear

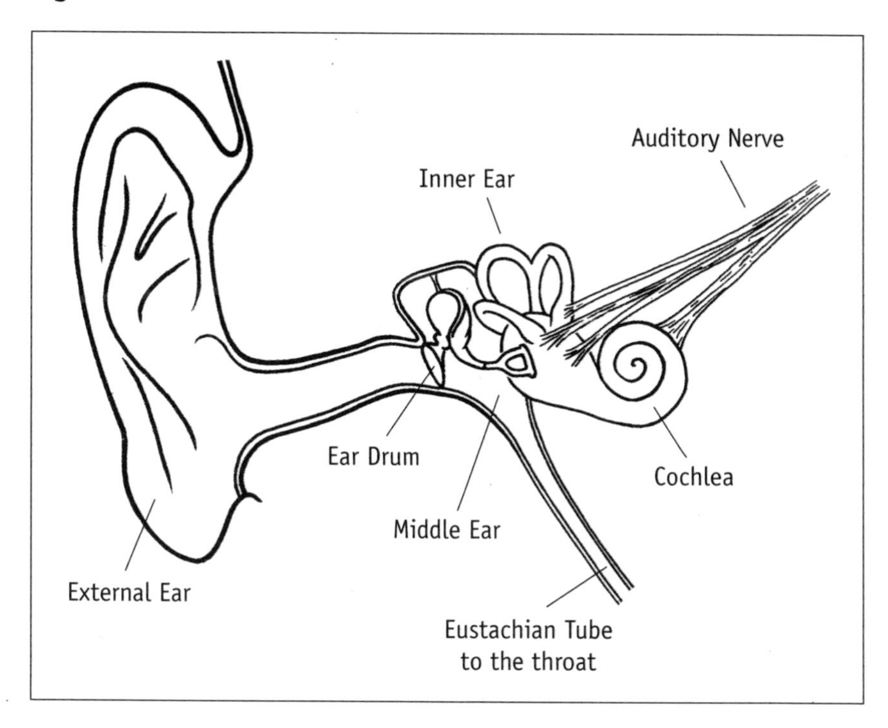

occur anywhere along this pathway. As with visual problems, regular screening for hearing problems is important. Again the earlier the identification of a problem the better the outlook after treatment. **If concerned a doctor's opinion should always be sought.** An ear specialist's assessment may be required.

Hearing loss: Hearing loss will affect virtually all people with Down syndrome at some point in their lives. *Any* degree of hearing loss can be described as deafness. There are two common forms of hearing loss: **conductive hearing loss** (where sound does not reach the inner ear appropriately) and **sensorineural hearing loss** (problems with the cochlea or with the auditory nerve carrying impulses to the brain area). A person can have both types at the same time.

Causes: The commonest causes are impacted wax in the ear canal, 'glue ear' (below), and changes in the structures of the ear with age (presbycusis). Other important causes include recurrent middle ear infections (below), a perforated eardrum with damage to the middle ear, an object in the ear canal, and rarely, disease affecting the auditory nerve.

Symptoms and signs: Often mild to moderate hearing loss can go unrecognised. Hearing loss may be suspected if there is failure to respond to sound, problems in learning, being withdrawn, being quiet, lacking response to communication and an increase in behavioural or emotional problems.

Investigations: There will need to be an assessment for hearing loss after any wax present in the ear canal is removed. Hearing tests should be, where possible, by an audiologist (a person who assesses hearing) with experience in seeing people with a learning disability. Good assessment at all ages of people with Down syndrome can be difficult because of poor co-operation, small ear canals, and excessive wax. Occasionally mild sedation may be required.

Complications: Problems that can occur include: impaired speech and language, poor educational progress, impaired social functioning, behavioural and emotional problems. A misdiagnosis of an emotional disorder (for example depression or dementia) can occur.

Treatment and prevention: Early detection is essential to prevent serious handicaps. Conductive deafness can often be improved. Provision of a hearing aid from a specialist centre (Chapter 5) is often necessary (see hearing aids below). Compliance may be poor and considerable time and effort may be needed to persuade the person to wear an aid. Recurrent upper respiratory tract infections may be considered to be treated with decongestants, large doses of vitamin C and antibiotics. Sensorineural deafness is usually permanent and is more difficult to help but some people can benefit from a cochlear implant. There are however other ways to improve understanding. These are mainly by improving face-to-face communication, involving a speech and language therapist and/or by learning communication signs and symbols. Support for carers and informing day placement staff of the deafness is an important part of the management.

Earache: Pain in or around the ear.

Causes: Usually caused by an inflammation or ear infection (below) of the outer ear or of the middle ear. Other causes can include 'glue ear' (below) and referred pain from the teeth, tonsils or sinuses.

Symptoms and signs: Earache can present as pain in the ear, discharge from the ear, person pulling or rubbing ear. Other more general features are being distressed, disturbed sleep, refusing to eat, showing emotional or behavioural problems.

Investigations: There needs to be a careful examination of the ear and also the nose and throat.

Complications: Usually none. But if due to an infection, this can spread and can lead to conductive deafness (see hearing loss above).

Treatment: Need to find and treat the cause. Painkillers (for example paracetamol) can relieve any discomfort. Any infection needs prompt treatment with antibiotics.

Impacted ear wax (cerumen): This is due to the build up of a yellow-brown secretion produced by glands in the outer ear. This is a normal product which usually helps to keep the ear canal clean.

Causes: The excessive production of ear wax is common in people with Down syndrome. Due also to the presence of smaller ear canals build up of wax is likely, with the risk of impaction increasing with age.

Symptoms and signs: Commonly hearing loss (above), feeling of being 'bunged up' and irritation in ear.

Investigations: An ear examination will reveal impacted wax.

Complications: Can result in conductive hearing loss (above).

Treatment: Hard wax should be removed by a professional person by softening of wax with oil (several days) and then flushing out with warm water (syringing of ears). Occasionally a probe may be needed to remove wax. The insertion of objects by carers can lead to wax being trapped further down the ear canal or can lead to a perforation of the ear drum.

Ear infections:

Causes: An acute infection is due to a viral or bacterial infection. A chronic ear infection often presents as a perforated ear drum with discharge from the middle ear.

Symptoms and signs: An acute infection presents with earache (above), discharge from ear, hearing loss (above), inflamed ear, fever and usually a history of a recent cold or of flu. A chronic condition usually has no redness, no bulging, no pain but presents as 'glue ear' (below). Emotional or behavioural changes can be the first sign of an ear infection.

Investigations: An ear, nose and throat examination is necessary. A hearing assessment may be necessary if hearing loss persists.

Complications: Recurrent infections can lead to a 'glue ear' (below) or hearing loss (above).

Treatment: Need to treat the underlying cause. Paracetamol can be given for pain. Antibiotics and decongestant drugs may be prescribed. Hearing will need to be monitored.

Glue ear: A build-up of thick and sticky fluid ('glue') in the middle ear. Common, especially in children.

Causes: A blockage of the Eustachian canal from the ear to the throat because of congestion during upper respiratory tract infections leading to a build up of 'glue-like' fluid in the middle ear.

Symptoms and signs: (See deafness above).

Investigations: An ear, nose and throat examination. A hearing assessment will be required.

Complications: Can result in persistent hearing loss (above).

Treatment and prevention: Decongestant medication taken for several weeks may be of benefit but may have limited effect. Surgical intervention can be given with use of grommets and T tubes (tiny plastic washers inserted into ear drum) to let air into the ear. This prevents the accumulation and development of the fluid. Insertion of tubes remains controversial and specialist advice should be sought. Follow-up after insertion is required to monitor improvement. Grommets and tubes are designed to extrude as part of the natural cleaning process of the ear and review is necessary to assess the state of the middle ear when the tubes fall out. Hearing aids or removal of adenoids and/or tonsils may also be considered. Ear plugs should be worn at times of bathing and swimming to prevent water entering the middle ear through the tube.

Hearing aids

Hearing aids are used to amplify sound to the middle ear. Their use can improve both conductive and sensorineural hearing loss. They are usually worn behind the ear or in the ear. Expert advice is needed about fitting and help to comply with wearing them (see hearing aid services – chapter 5). Ongoing training and support from a speech and language therapist may be necessary. Advice to parents, carers and teachers on how to improve communication is important.

Chapter 8

HEART AND CIRCULATION

Heart problems are very common in people with Down syndrome. Nowadays such problems are usually detected before or soon after birth. Problems can however persist into adulthood or start later in life and give cause for concern. As for children, all adults with Down syndrome should continue to have ongoing monitoring of the health of their heart. Regular screening for heart and circulation problems at all ages should be undertaken. **If any symptoms or signs suggest a heart problem, a medical opinion must be sought.**

Pulse rate (Abnormal): The pulse rate is detected by pressing one or more fingers against the skin over an artery (usually at the wrist, neck or groin). The rate can be measured as beats per minute and corresponds to the heart rate. The pulse rate is usually between 60 and 100 beats per minute when a person is resting. For an adult in the general population the average pulse rate is 72 beats/minute, but for adults with Down syndrome it is lower at 65 beats/minute. An abnormal heart rate (fast or slow), abnormal rhythm or a weak pulse can be a sign of heart disease, obstruction of the blood circulation or of general ill-health.

Causes: The heart rate can be higher (tachycardia, over 85 beats per minute) due to exercise, emotion, fever, anaemia, hyperthyroidism and heart disease. It can be lower (bradycardia, less than 50 beats per minute) due to hypothermia, hypothyroidism, drug therapy or heart disease.

Symptoms and signs: As well as a slow or fast heart rate there can be a number of other symptoms present. These include palpitations (a fluttering feeling in the chest), chest pain, fainting, breathlessness and poor exercise tolerance.

Investigations: These include examination of the health of the heart by electrocardiography (ECG, recording of the electrical currents of the heart) and echocardiography (ultrasound of the heart to produce moving images). Blood tests can also be undertaken to exclude illnesses that can affect the heart (eg thyroid disease, anaemia).

Complications: Problems may not occur but heart failure and hypotension (low blood pressure) are important complications to watch out for.

Treatment: Any treatment given will depend on the underlying cause and also if there are secondary problems. Usually reassurance and an explanation of what is happening is all that is needed. However, medication to slow or increase the heart rate or to reduce the work on the heart is usually the main form of treatment if intervention is required. Only rarely may a heart pacemaker need to be fitted if there is no benefit with medication or the heart problem is life-threatening.

Blood pressure (Abnormal): Blood pressure (BP) is the pressure exerted by the flow of blood through the arteries of the body. Pressure can vary considerably during different stresses put on the heart. The highest pressure point (systolic BP) is pressure created by the contraction of the heart muscle and the lowest point (diastolic BP) is that present when the heart muscle is in relaxation. No single BP is normal for all individuals in all circumstances. The *average* BP for a resting adult in the general population is a systolic BP of 110–120mmHg and a diastolic BP of 75–80mmHg. For an adult with Down syndrome it is a systolic BP of 105–115mmHg and a diastolic BP of 70–75mmHg respectively. For children and young adults the BP is lower. There is a gradual increase in BP with age (Figure 6). A normal BP can vary for many reasons including age, anxiety, exercise and with the size of the cuff used.

Hypertension (high blood pressure [BP]): This is an uncommon condition in adults with Down syndrome. The BP must be estimated on several occasions before it can be declared

Figure 6: Blood pressure by age for Down syndrome population

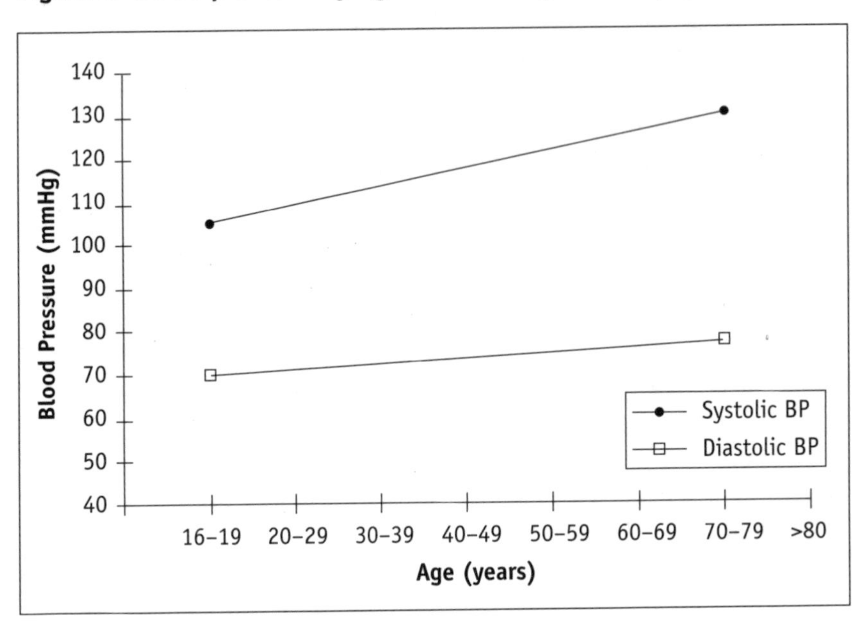

abnormally elevated (hypertensive). Hypertension for adults with Down syndrome is a systolic BP greater than 90mmHg plus age in years and/or a diastolic BP greater than 90mmHg.

Causes: In the vast majority of people no cause is found but in a significant minority obesity, heart disease, kidney disease, gland disorders and drugs can be factors.

Symptoms and signs: Often there are no symptoms. Severe hypertension can present with headaches, shortness of breath, dizziness or confusion.

Investigations: Initially there is a need to measure the BP on several occasions to confirm a persistently high level. A general physical examination particularly including the heart, eyes and urine is necessary to exclude any organ damage. Blood tests will be necessary to investigate for a possible underlying cause and to exclude kidney damage.

Complications: Not inevitable but if uncontrolled for some time can lead to heart disease, kidney failure, a stroke or impaired vision.

Treatment and prevention: Regular BP checks for all adults with Down syndrome but in particular for those with a previous high level should be undertaken. This can be done by the person's GP. A reduction in weight, reduced salt intake, exercise, relaxation and stopping smoking have been shown to be beneficial. Antihypertensive drugs (eg diuretics, beta-blockers) may be necessary. Any drug treatment will need to be monitored closely by a doctor and once started is usually life-long.

Heart problems: The heart is basically a pump made of muscle ensuring that blood is moved around the body. There are four chambers, two at the top (left and right atrium) and two at the bottom (left and right ventricles). Muscle walls (septa) and valves keep the chambers separate (Figure 7). Blood from the body collects in the right atrium, enters the right ventricle, is pumped to the lungs to collect oxygen, returns to the left atrium, enters the left

Figure 7: Structure of the Heart

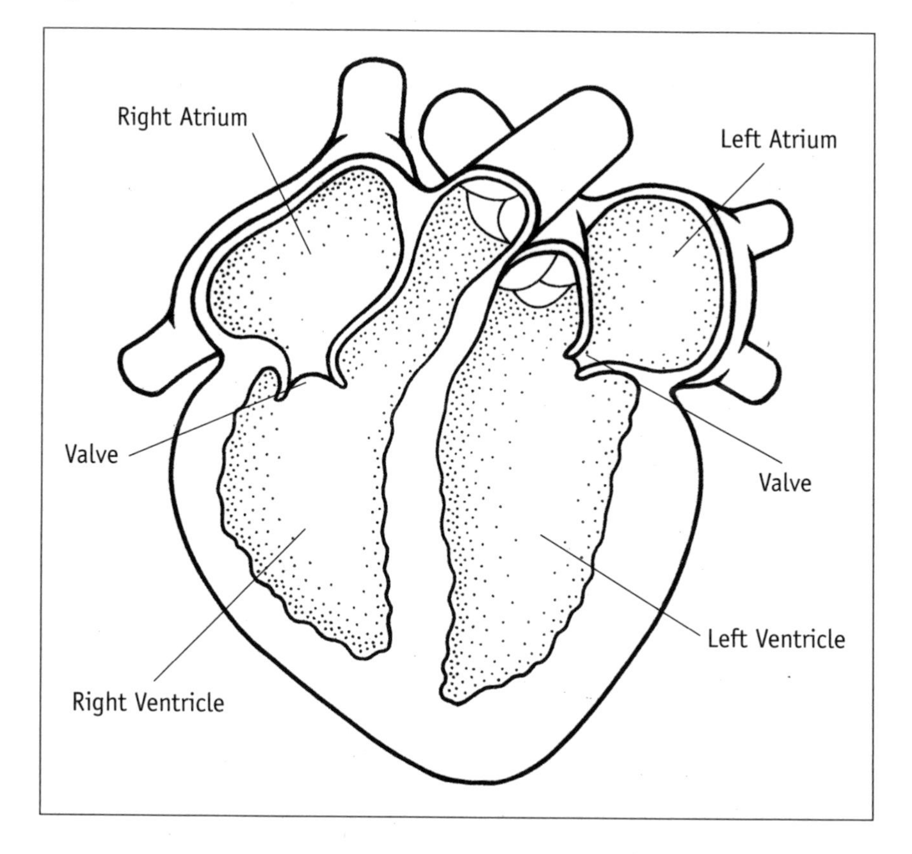

ventricle and is pumped to the body, only to later return again to the right atrium. Problems can occur with a 'hole' being present in the muscle wall dividing the chambers (see heart lesions below), in the function of the heart valves, in the muscle of the heart or with the vessels returning or taking blood away from the heart.

Causes: (See specific heart lesions below). The vast majority of abnormalities are present at birth and should be detected at birth as part of a health screening programme. Some problems can present in later life because of a deterioration of childhood abnormalities or as part of weakness in the muscles of the heart valves or following untreated hypertension (above).

Symptoms and signs/complications: Valve defects and 'holes' in the heart impair the efficiency of the heart by causing blood to flow in different directions. This leads to different chambers working harder than expected which can in turn lead to heart failure (below) or lung disease (see chapter 9). The greater the defect, the greater the stress experienced by the heart.

Investigations: The severity and type of heart problem needs to be detected. Tests to detect any damage to the heart or lungs include blood tests, a chest x-ray, electrocardiography (ECG, the assessment of the electrical activity of the heart) and an echocardiography (ultra-sound of the heart).

Treatment and prevention: Routine screening for heart problems should be undertaken. Early diagnosis and management is essential for future good health and long-life. Treatment will depend on the cause and on the severity of any problem.

Specific heart lesions: Virtually all heart lesions in people with Down syndrome become apparent at or soon after birth. They should all be detected and treated if necessary during early childhood. However such problems can persist into adulthood or occur when a child with Down syndrome becomes an adult (eg mitral valve prolapse). **Antibiotic cover must be given to any person with Down syndrome who is known to have a heart lesion and is about to undergo treatment which may lead to bacteria entering the bloodstream (see endocarditis below).**

Ventricular septal defect (VSD): This is a 'hole' in the muscle wall separating the two ventricles, which occurs in approximately 30%

of all heart defects. A VSD results in blood flow from the left ventricle to the right ventricle. This can lead to high blood pressure in the blood vessels to the lungs. A VSD can occasionally be part of a condition called 'tetralogy of Fallot' (see below). Small VSDs may close spontaneously and cause no problems. Larger defects or those that lead to symptoms will need surgical closure.

Atrial septal defect (ASD): Is associated with blood flow from the left atrium to the right atrium. Usually an ASD does not lead to significant problems but individuals can be prone to chest infections, breathlessness, tiredness, palpitations and an abnormal heart beat. The occurrence of a VSD and an ASD together is termed '*atrioventricular septal defect* (AVSD)' and is quite common in people with Down syndrome. Small defects may close spontaneously or cause no significant problem but larger defects will need surgical intervention to close the defect.

Patent ductus arteriosus: Occurs in approximately 5–10% of heart defects. The ductus arteriosus is a blood vessel near the heart which normally closes within 48 hours after birth but if closure does not occur it remains open ('patent'). Often it can be a large opening and be associated with other defects. If untreated it can result in blood from the main blood vessel taking blood away from the heart to the rest of the body (aorta) flowing into the main artery of the lungs and leading to hypertension in the vessels of the lungs. If found to be causing problems it will need surgical intervention.

Aortic coarctation: is a narrowing of the main blood vessel (the aorta) taking blood away from the heart. Symptoms are often absent but hypertension in the upper part of the body can develop. May require surgical intervention.

Mitral valve prolapse (MVP): This is a malfunction of the mitral valve (the valve that controls blood flow from the left atrium to the left ventricle). May develop in later life. Mild MVP is common in about one-third of people with Down syndrome. Mitral valve prolapse may be associated with an ASD (above) and keratoconus (chapter 6). Usually heart lesions are detected by the presence of a heart murmur or when they lead to heart failure (below). Screening for MVP by echocardiography (ultrasound of the heart to produce moving images) has been recommended by some doctors. If severe, surgical intervention will be necessary.

Tetralogy of Fallot: A group of heart lesions present at birth. Should be detected at birth or early childhood but problems may persist into adulthood.

Causes: Include a VSD (see heart lesions above), narrowing of blood vessel to lungs, right ventricle enlargement and abnormalities of the aorta (main blood vessel taking blood away from the heart). Leads to mixing of blood within the heart.

Symptoms and signs: Common symptoms include tiredness, cyanosis (morbid bluish discolourization of skin and lips), squatting after exercise and the presence of several heart murmurs.

Investigations: (See heart problems above).

Complications: Can result in heart failure (see below), polycythemia (an increase in the amount of haemoglobin in the blood; see chapter 15) and can lead to early death.

Treatment and prevention: After exercise the squatting position can help. Need to treat any resulting heart failure and any fevers promptly. Adults with Down syndrome with this condition should have been treated in childhood with surgery to close and correct defects.

Heart failure: A condition where the heart is unable to work properly in pumping blood around the body. Results in inadequate oxygen supply to tissues.

Causes: There are a number of causes of heart failure but the most important ones for adults with Down syndrome are heart lesions (above), thyroid disorders (chapter 14) and lung disease (chapter 9). Heart failure may affect only the left side of the heart, only the right side or both sides (called 'congestive heart failure').

Symptoms and signs: Symptoms may not be present until permanent damaged has occurred. Coughing, fast heart beat, sweating, paleness, chest infections, fainting, fatigue, breathlessness, chest deformities and an enlarged heart may be detected. On examination there may be a heart murmur, weight gain, swollen legs, laboured breathing with excessive chest movement and a rapid heart rate. Fluid in the lungs may be present. An enlarged liver or polycythemia may be seen.

Investigations: (See heart problems above).

Complications: If untreated can lead to early death.

Treatment: Medication (eg diuretics, beta-blockers, digoxin) may be given to treat the heart failure. Surgery may be considered for replacement of defective valves or correction of heart lesions. Antibiotic cover when going to the dentist or going for any kind of surgery is necessary to prevent any infection which may get into the bloodstream from settling in the heart (see endocarditis below).

Endocarditis: An infection within the heart. The infection is usually of the heart valves or at the site of a heart lesion.

Causes: Usually bacteria from the mouth or from the urinary system at time of dental treatment or after an urinary infection or procedure.

Symptoms and signs: Fever, night sweats, weight loss, weakness, changing murmur, skin lesions, microscopic signs of blood in urine, attacks of abdominal pain (due to clots dislodged from heart), heart failure (see above).

Investigations: Blood screen for anaemia or evidence of inflammation, urine screen for blood being passed in urine, blood analysis to isolate infective organism, echocardiogram (recording of an ultra-sound of the heart) and chest x-ray to detect damage to heart.

Complications: Can lead to heart failure, clumps of bacteria can be dislodged from the heart and can block off the blood supply to other organs eg kidneys, spleen, lungs. Can be a fatal condition.

Treatment and prevention: Any underlying infection must be treated with antibiotics. Surgery may be necessary if damage to any heart valve has occurred. **Treatment with antibiotics one hour before any procedure which may lead to bacteria entering the bloodstream (eg dental treatment) in individuals with heart defect is essential to prevent endocarditis.** Good dental hygiene is important (Chapter 13).

Eisenmenger complex: This is a disorder affecting the heart and lungs together due to a long standing heart lesion (ASD, VSD or patent ductus arteriosus – above).

Cause: The presence of a heart lesion can lead over time to damage to the blood vessels in the lungs. This can increase resistance to blood passing through the lungs which in turn leads to increased work put on the heart and results in heart problems.

Symptoms and signs: Frequent symptoms include a morbid blueness of the skin and lips (cyanosis), breathlessness, tiredness, chest pain, swollen legs, fainting and headaches.

Investigations: Undertaken to confirm the disorder and to detect degree of damage present. Include an echocardiogram (recording of an ultra-sound of the heart), a chest x-ray, cardiac catheterization (insertion of a fine tube into a blood vessel in the groin and passed into the heart). Blood tests to measure the thickness of blood and the blood haemoglobin concentration.

Complications: Can result in permanent heart damage, heart failure, polycythemia (chapter 15).

Treatment: May need to remove blood (similar to what is done when giving a blood donation) to reduce the thickness of the blood and to reduce stress on the heart. Regular monitoring by a heart specialist doctor to prevent future lung damage is important. A heart and lung transplantation may be required if the condition becomes severe.

Chapter 9

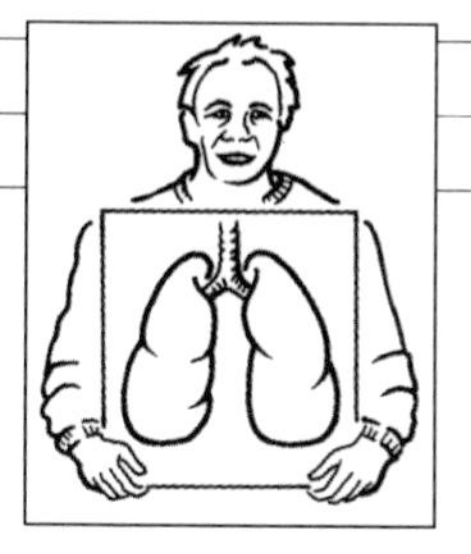

RESPIRATORY PROBLEMS

Breathing and airway related problems can vary from minor but irritating colds, to life threatening respiratory failure. Chest infections and breathing problems are more common in people with Down syndrome than the general population due to the underlying differences in structure and function of the airways. Frequent but minor conditions are discussed as well as the less common but more serious health problems. It must be borne in mind that chest infections still remain a major cause of death in adults with Down syndrome. **If breathing or swallowing is difficult, symptoms are severe or prolonged, a medical opinion should always be sought.**

Common cold:

Causes: This is usually due to a viral infection which can be highly infective in the early stages. The spread of the virus occurs by inhaling droplets containing the virus which are coughed or sneezed into air. More common in the winter months.

Symptoms and signs: Common symptoms include a slight temperature, tiredness, sneezing, sore nose and throat, watering eyes, headache and nasal discharge (watery initially but later thick and 'green').

Investigations: Usually none needed. If persistent may need blood tests to detect evidence of infection and a sputum analysis for evidence and type of infection.

Complications: Can lead to the infection spreading to other areas; in particular the upper airways, sinuses and middle ear.

Treatment and prevention: Most colds usually clear within one week. Warm humid room, regular paracetamol for aches and pains, bed rest, plenty of fluid intake, continuing to eat some food and steam inhalation can be of benefit. If a cold continues to persist, if symptoms are severe or a secondary bacterial infection occurs, antibiotics may be required. Over-the-counter remedies usually include a painkiller, decongestant and an antihistamine (a drug that blocks the action of histamine which is involved in producing an allergic reaction eg astemizole, terfenadine and which may relieve the symptoms). There is no definite prevention known but large quantities of Vitamin C may help.

Nosebleed (epistaxis): Bleeding, usually from the blood vessels on the nasal septum.

Causes: Most nosebleeds have no particular cause. Can be due to hypertension (chapter 8), inflammation of the nasal cavity, general bleeding disorder.

Symptoms and signs: As well as bleeding may be other symptoms associated with underlying cause.

Investigation: Usually none required. If persists investigate for underlying cause.

Complications: Person may develop shock (rarely).

Treatment: Nurse person in sitting up position. Firm pressure to be applied to nostrils by finger and thumb for at least 10 minutes. Ice-pack can be applied to bridge of nose. If bleeding persists will need medical attention where anaesthetic spray can be applied to constrict blood vessels and nasal pack inserted to stop further bleeding.

Sore throat (pharyngitis): An inflammation of the throat between the tonsils and the upper part of the windpipe.

Causes: Often part of a common cold (above). Caused usually by a virus but sometimes can be bacterial.

Symptoms and signs: As well as a sore throat, the top of the mouth can be reddened and tonsils inflamed and swollen. There may be discomfort on swallowing, slight fever or earache. The lymph nodes in the neck may be enlarged.

Investigations: (See common cold above). If persists a throat swab can be taken to isolate the cause of the inflammation.

Complications: Can occasionally spread to involve other parts of the airways. Epidemics can occur.

Treatment: The disease is self-limiting and symptomatic relief is usually all that is required. Gargling with warm salt water, avoiding lying flat and use of painkillers can help. Antiseptic lozenges and sprays can make things worse. For severe or persistent tonsillitis antibiotics may be required.

Hayfever (seasonal rhinitis):

Cause: Commonly an allergic reaction usually to tree or grass pollen or mould spores. More common in young adults, in people with asthma and/or with eczema and usually worst in June and July when pollen counts are higher.

Symptoms and signs: Include nasal irritation, sneezing, watery runny nose, itching of eyes or top of mouth or ear.

Investigations: Detailed history is often all that is needed to make a diagnosis. Skin-prick testing for allergies and an assessment of immune status with blood tests can be undertaken.

Complications: Usually none but breathing and feeding difficulties can occur.

Treatment and prevention: Best to avoid or reduce contact with allergen. Antihistamines (group of drugs that block the action of histamine which is necessary to produce an allergic reaction eg astemizole, terfenadine) can be prescribed. Decongestants, steroids, anti-inflammatory drugs may also be given. Older antihistamines are associated with sedation.

Constant runny nose (perennial rhinitis): A constant nasal discharge throughout the year.

Causes: Allergic (to house dust mite, pollen grains, domestic animals, moulds) and non-allergic types.

Symptoms and signs: Sneezing, watery runny nose, nasal blockage, loss of smell and taste, sinusitis.

Investigation/complications/treatment and prevention: (See hayfever above).

Adenoids (enlarged): Swollen lymph glands found at the back of the nose. These glands are present to fight infections.

Causes: A viral or a bacterial infection.
Symptoms and signs: Snoring, chronic discharge from nose, cough.
Complications: Can lead to ear infections, 'glue ear' (chapter 7), obstructive sleep apnoea (below).
Treatment: Need to clear any discharge from the nose with steam inhalation and if necessary a course of antibiotics. For recurrent cases surgical removal of the adenoids (adenoidectomy) may be necessary.

Sinusitis: An inflammation of the sinuses (air cavities found near the nose within the skull).
Causes: Usually following a nasal infection.
Symptoms and signs: Increased nasal discharge, headaches, tenderness over cheeks, feeling of fullness in affected area, throbbing ache, loss of smell. Presence of a green/yellow nasal discharge suggests a bacterial infection.
Investigations: Usually none required but an x-ray examination of the sinuses can show evidence of the inflammation.
Complications: Breathing and feeding difficulties possible. Can in rare cases lead to meningitis.
Treatment: Persistent problems with clear drainage suggests a possible allergic reaction and antihistamines or decongestants may be of benefit. Steam drainage can be helpful. A green-yellow discharge would suggest the need for antibiotics. Surgical drainage is occasionally considered.

Asthma: An inflammation of the small airways making breathing difficult.
Causes: Can be a history of problems in the family. Often no cause found. Can be due to allergies eg pollen, house dust, animal fur, feathers, atmospheric pollution, drugs, infections, emotional upsets. Usually starts in childhood and can clear with increasing age.
Symptoms and signs: Recurrent attacks of wheezing, shortness of breath, cough, tightness in chest, a fast heart rate. Often worse at night. In severe attacks breathing can be very difficult with considerable distress and anxiety, episodes of lips becoming 'blue' (cyanosis).
Investigations: May not be necessary but can test how well lungs are working by blowing hard into a small instrument which measures

lung volume (peak-flow meter). Blood and sputum tests can be undertaken to detect any infection. A chest X-ray can detect any damage to lungs. An allergen provocation test may be considered to find the allergy if suspected.

Complications: Includes severe breathing difficulty (status asthmaticus), collapsed lung, respiratory failure. If untreated a severe attack can cause death.

Treatment and prevention: Medication usually in the form of an inhaler (sodium cromglycate, steroids) is used to prevent an attack by being taken on a regular basis. More active medication can also be given at the time of an acute attack. Antibiotics occasionally required. Recurrent attacks should be investigated for other underlying problems eg foreign body in airways, immune deficiency, difficulty in administration of medication. **Can be a medical emergency. If there is severe cyanosis or severe breathing problems request paramedical help.**

Bronchitis: An inflammation of the airways to the lungs.

Causes: Often viral but can be complicated by a bacterial infection. Smoking and air pollutants can predispose to infections.

Acute symptoms and signs: Irritating unproductive cough, discomfort and tightness in chest, wheezing and shortness of breath, a cough which is later productive of yellow or green sputum, mild fever.

Chronic symptoms and signs: Several episodes of cough with production of sputum, wheeze and breathlessness. Frequent infections and exacerbation can occur in poor weather.

Investigations: Can undertake an assessment of lung function with peak-flow meters, chest x-ray to show any infection, sputum analysis for evidence of infection. If necessary, blood tests to measure amount of oxygen and carbon dioxide in bloodstream.

Complications: Can occasionally lead to pneumonia (below) or heart failure (chapter 8).

Treatment and prevention: Need to avoid smoking (active and passive) and air pollutants. The inhalation of steam and drinking plenty of fluids can help. Medication to improve breathing and antibiotics for any infection may be prescribed. Physiotherapy and oxygen can be given to improve lung function.

Influenza: A viral infection of the airways which can affect adults with Down syndrome more seriously than adults in the general population.

Causes: A particular type of virus which is often associated with local milder outbreaks. However worldwide epidemics can occur. The virus can be spread by inhalation of infected droplets sneezed or coughed into air. Three types of virus (A,B, and C).

Symptoms and signs: The incubation period is of 1–3 days. Sudden fever, shivering and shaking in limbs, severe headache follows, soreness of throat and persistent dry cough, muscle ache, fatigue, loss of appetite. Getting back to normal activities is usually achieved gradually. Secondary bacterial infections can occur.

Investigations: Usually none necessary but can measure body response to virus by means of blood test.

Complications: Can lead to pneumonia (below), sinusitis (above), middle ear infection (chapter 7), post-infection depression or deterioration in previously well-controlled mental illness.

Treatment and prevention: (See common cold above). A vaccine can usually be given to prevent someone getting the illness. Vaccines tend to be effective in 70% of cases but are often short-lasting. A vaccine should not be given if the person is allergic to egg protein.

Pneumonia: An inflammation of the lungs usually due to an infection. More common in older adults and adults with Down syndrome who have reduced immunity.

Causes: Usually a viral or bacterial infection.

Symptoms and signs: Common symptoms include a high temperature, chest pain, dry cough, rusty-coloured sputum, fast breathing and difficulty in breathing.

Investigations: Will require a chest x-ray, sputum analysis and a blood screen for evidence and type of infection.

Complications: Can lead to an inflammation around the lungs, fluid collection or an abscess (collection of pus) in the lungs, a collapsed lung, respiratory failure and spread of infection into the bloodstream (septicaemia). If not treated pneumonia can in some cases lead to death.

Treatment: Can usually be managed at home but may require hospitalisation. Plenty of fluids, physiotherapy to chest, analgesia (paracetamol, aspirin) is required. Will need hospital care with lung ventilation in severe cases. Anti-infection drugs can be given.

Obstructive sleep apnoea (OSA): A condition in which the airway at the back of the throat is sucked closed when breathing in during sleep. The airflow is interrupted for usually more than 10 seconds.

Causes: Often no single factor found. Associated with poor muscle tone, small upper airways, frequent chest infections, obesity, hypothyroidism, enlarged tonsils or adenoids, nasal obstruction and drugs affecting respiration eg sedatives and strong analgesia.

Symptoms and signs: Loud snoring, daytime sleeping, restless sleep, morning headache, mouth breathing, nocturnal choking, poor concentration, irritability and behavioural problems.

Investigations: Need to confirm an abnormal night-time breathing pattern. Videotaping of night-time breathing is important. 'Oximetry-testing' is required to confirm the disorder. This is where the brain waves, blood oxygen levels, muscle tone and movement and other bodily signs are measured whilst the person sleeps.

Complications: Can cause hypertension or heart failure (chapter 8), a stroke, or lung disease.

Treatment and prevention: Need to treat any underlying factors (eg lose weight), avoid sedating drugs, avoid sleep deprivation. Antidepressants (group of drugs used to treat depression eg amitripytline, fluoxetine) can help in milder cases. May need to give what is termed 'continuous positive airway pressure' which involves giving of oxygen and air under pressure via a tightly fitted face mask. A tonsillectomy and/or an adenoidectomy (surgical removal of the adenoids) may be necessary.

Chapter 10

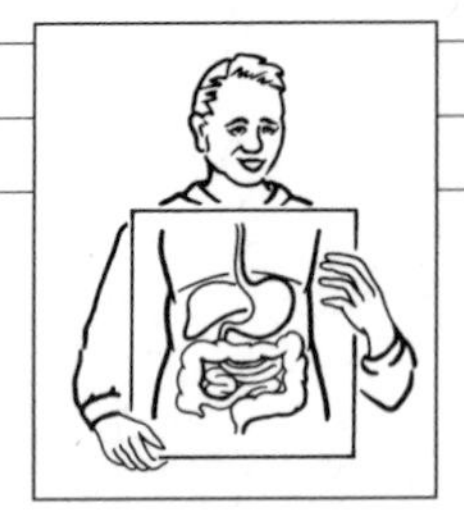

DIGESTIVE SYSTEM

Digestive problems can be present at birth and persist throughout the lifetime of a person with Down syndrome or develop later during adulthood. Problems may arise with the structure or with the function of the gut (Figure 8). Families and carers need to be vigilant for any symptoms or signs suggesting an underlying serious problem such as blood in stools, marked weight loss, severe abdominal pain. Minor as well as the more serious health problems that can occur in adults with Down syndrome are discussed. **Persistent, severe symptoms or deterioration in health necessitate a medical assessment.**

Choking:

Causes: An obstruction of the throat usually with food, drink or swallowed object (peanut, bead) leading to difficulty in breathing.

Symptoms and signs: Person may look 'blue', speechless, in distress.

Complication: If not managed immediately can lead to death.

Treatment: Grasp person around abdomen from behind and squeeze hard inwards and upwards to eject food. **Call for emergency help if first aid unsuccessful.**

Vomiting: Can be associated with wanting to vomit (nausea) and effort to vomit (retching).

Causes: Commonest reasons are travelling sickness, ear or urine infection, emotional upset, general illness or side-effects of medication. The more important medical causes related to the digestive system include constipation, bowel obstruction, food

Figure 8: Digestive System

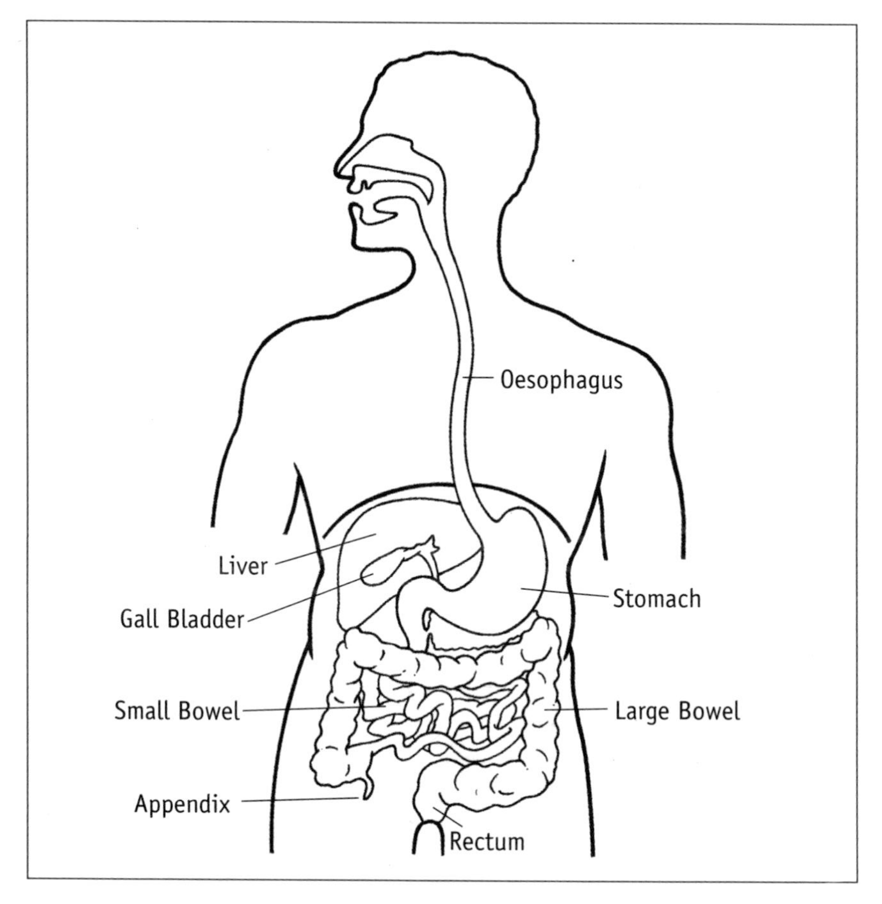

poisoning, gastroenteritis, coeliac disease (below) appendicitis and an ulcer. In these conditions vomiting is usually associated with abdominal pain. Other causes to consider include migraine, meningitis, diabetes, metabolic problems, over-eating and self-induced vomiting.

Symptoms and signs: Looking pale and sweating can occur prior to vomiting. Other features are associated with the underlying cause.

Investigations: Depend on the likely cause. Can include blood and urine tests for infection, x-ray examination and an endoscopy (passing of flexible tube through mouth down into the digestive system to view inside) to detect any abdominal problem.

Complications: If persistent can lead to imbalance in body electrolytes (specific chemicals in blood required for good health) and dehydration. Specific complications may be associated with a given cause.

Treatment: If obvious non-serious cause just need to monitor. No food or drink during episodes of vomiting. Clear fluids given initially. Drugs (called anti-emetics eg metoclopramide) can be given to stop the vomiting. Will need to treat underlying cause eg infection with antibiotics, constipation with laxatives, reduce/stop medication if side effect of medication. **If vomiting is severe or blood present see doctor.**

Eating problems: Eating problems are common in people with Down syndrome.

Causes: These relate to the social or emotional situation, as part of the stubborn personality of some people with Down syndrome, or as part of a physical or emotional disorder eg obsessive disorder (chapter 16).

Symptoms and signs: Frequent feeding problems include refusal to eat textured food, chewing difficulties, eating only specific foods, slow to finish a meal, throwing food away and hoarding food.

Investigations: Where there have been no previous problems with feeding, an underlying physical or emotional cause such as a problem with swallowing, constipation, depression, an obsessional disorder (chapter 16) should be investigated. Need to monitor weight. A dietician's or a psychologist's assessment of the eating habit may be necessary.

Complications: Weight loss (below), behavioural problems, constipation and nutritional deficiency (chapter 2) can occur. Considerable stress can be caused to carers.

Treatment and prevention: Education about appropriate food intake, making mealtimes distinct and inviting, encouraging eating with attention and/or special favourite foods after completion of meals should be recommended. Training in cooking skills, dieting and exercise can have considerable benefit. For adults with behavioural problems early intervention from a dietician or psychologist can be beneficial. If an underlying emotional disorder is present (depression, obsessional disorder – chapter 16) then treatment by a psychiatrist may be necessary. Carer support and ongoing monitoring of the weight and calorie intake is important. Supplementation with megavitamin therapy is **not** recommended.

Weight loss: It is important to compare the weight of a person with Down syndrome not only to people in the general population but also to that of other people with Down syndrome of the same age and sex (chapter 2). It is also important to compare the present weight to previous weight measurements.

Cause: The level of exercise and calorie intake will affect weight loss. Dieting and refusal to eat are intentional causes. Unintentional weight loss can be due to reduced appetite as a result of abdominal discomfort, physical ill-health, depression or dementia (chapter 16). Weight loss with a good appetite still present can be due to hyperthyroidism or diabetes (chapter 15), an infection, abdominal disease and rarely cancer.

Symptoms and signs: Evidence suggesting weight loss other than by weighing may be clothes becoming loose, comments from others, looking physically or emotionally unwell. Other symptoms may be associated with a particular cause.

Investigations: Depends on cause and severity. May need a general medical investigation to determine any underlying physical or psychological cause. Tests include urine or stool analysis, blood screen for inflammation or infection, endoscopic examination (means of looking directly into digestive system by using flexible tube), x-ray and ultrasound assessments (a procedure where sound waves are transmitted to the body and the reflection [echo] is detected using detectors. Echoes are converted by a computer to pictures).

Complications: Usually none unless severe sudden weight loss. Secondary problems may be associated with underlying cause.

Treatment and Prevention: Need to treat any underlying cause. Need to increase the calorie intake and reduce exercise. Advice and support from a dietician may be necessary.

Abdominal Pain: 'Tummy ache' is a common complaint in people with a learning disability.

Cause: Can be related to emotional upset, as part of a general illness or caused by a local abdominal problem. When due to gastrointestinal problems common causes include constipation (below), overeating and stomach irritation. Can be because of some other more serious abdominal problem (eg blockage to bowels – see below).

Symptoms and signs: Site, intensity, duration, character, aggravating and relieving factors and associated symptoms is important information relating to the pain. A central dull abdominal pain is usually due to stomach irritation (eg increased gastric acidity, peptic ulcer disease). Right upper abdomen pain can be due to gallbladder or biliary tract inflammation. Lower abdominal pain can be due to bladder infection, bowel problems, or gynaecological problems. An adult with Down syndrome may not be able to vocalise any discomfort but present with emotional or behavioural problems.

Investigations: (See weight loss above).

Complications: Can lead to marked behaviour and/or emotional disturbance. Secondary to underlying cause.

Treatment: Reassurance can often be all that is required. Recurrent attacks of mild pain may settle with simple painkillers, a milky drink, a hot-water bottle and bed-rest. More serious causes will need specific management and if pain is severe or persistent will need a medical assessment.

Mouth Ulcers:

Causes: No one particular cause. Often unknown. Can be due to trauma, infection (for example herpes) associated with bowel disease, nutritional deficiencies, or drug therapy.

Symptoms and signs: May mimic toothache (chapter 13). Avoidance of contact with the ulcer when eating is common. Pain may be experienced on brushing teeth near the ulcer.

Complications: Usually none

Treatment: Application to the ulcer of a gel containing chlorhexidine (eg Corsodyl) or steroids can temporarily relieve pain. Need to see a dentist if persists longer than two weeks or if there is no response to simple measures.

Bowel obstruction: A blockage to the bowel preventing passage of contents along the full length of the bowel.

Causes: Many possible causes from a swallowed foreign body, problems in bowel motility to compression of the bowel from outside.

Symptoms and signs: Depends on the site of the obstruction but generally nausea and vomiting, abdominal pain, constipation, colic and swelling of the abdomen. Behavioural or emotional deterioration can be the first sign of a physical problem.

Investigations: Undertaken to find severity and cause. Common tests include an x-ray examination, blood screen for chemical imbalance, and an endoscopy (means of looking into the digestive system by using flexible tube).

Complications: Rare but a rupture of the bowel can occur leading to peritonitis (inflammation of the lining of the abdomen).

Treatment: Requires medical intervention. Treatment depends on cause, for example, if an object has been swallowed this will need to be removed, constipation will require either strong laxatives by mouth or a rectal enema. If simple measures fail may need admission to hospital for further treatment. This includes trying to reduce the abdominal distension with a tube (nasogastric tube) passed through nose into stomach to remove build up of gas, replacement of fluids lost and surgery to remove obstruction.

Constipation: Passage of small hard faeces infrequently and with difficulty. There is wide normal variation of bowel habit (several times/day to twice/week). A change from normal habit is important to note. It is a common problem in people with Down syndrome because of low muscle tone, reduced mobility and fussy diets.

Causes: Include inadequate fibre in diet, reduced fluid intake, lack of regular habits, lack of physical activity, diet, hypothyroidism (chapter 15), depression (chapter 16), side-effects of drugs, and bowel disease.

Symptoms and signs: Commonly include flatulence, bloating, abdominal pain, small hard stools, and over-flow diarrhoea. Behavioural disturbance can occur. Possibly associated with deterioration in epilepsy.

Investigations: If persists may require abdominal x-ray examinations and blood tests to exclude thyroid disease.

Complications: Bowel obstruction possible (above).

Treatment and prevention: High-fibre diet eg whole grain cereals, bran, raw fruits and vegetables, adequate fluid intake. Prunes can act as a laxative. Active exercise can aid movement of stool through the bowel. Regular bowel habits and good toileting skills are important. Glycerol suppositories, laxatives and enemas can be prescribed but prolonged use can impair normal functioning. Treat any underlying cause.

Diarrhoea: Frequently passed loose stools. There is a wide normal variation in bowel habit so a change from normal frequency is important. Watery large volume stools suggest a bowel infection (especially if bloody).

Causes: Include dietary causes, bowel infection, bowel disease, drugs, metabolic problems, faecal impaction, and emotional problems. Acute diarrhoea can occur for a few days, usually due to contaminated food or drink and settles without intervention. Chronic diarrhoea may be due to bowel disease, hyperthyroidism, irritable bowel disease, or from side-effects of medication.

Symptoms and signs: Include loose motions, cramp-like abdominal pain, distress, restlessness, weight loss, blood in stools and associated fever.

Investigations: May need further assessment including rectal examination, stool analysis to identify any infection, blood tests, x-ray examination or biopsy of bowel.

Complications: Dehydration in the elderly is possible and can present as drowsiness, unresponsiveness, glazed eyes, dry mouth and poor urine output. If severe dehydration occurs then hospital admission to rehydrate will be needed. Blood chemical imbalance can occur if diarrhoea is severe or prolonged.

Treatment: Replace fluid loss initially with clear water with dissolved sugar. No solids until diarrhoea settles. Start gradually to introduce food. Antidiarrhoea drugs (group of drugs used to stop diarrhoea either by forming bulk eg Kaolin mixture or reducing gut motility eg codeine phosphate) can be of help. Treat underlying cause.

Coeliac disease: Malabsorption syndrome. Usually diagnosed in childhood but can present at any age.

Causes: The body develops an allergy to 'gluten' protein found in wheat and cereal grains. The bowel wall becomes inflamed and lining becomes flat impairing absorption of foods and minerals.

Symptoms and signs: Abnormal stools (diarrhoea, foul smelling), swollen abdomen, irritability, anaemia, tiredness, malaise, abdominal pain, weight loss and vomiting.

Investigations: Blood test for specific indicators of coeliac disease called 'anti-gliadin antibodies'. Antibodies are proteins produced by the body's immune system which help to neutralise infecting agents such as bacteria or viruses. May need to undergo small bowel biopsy, blood tests for anaemia.

Complications: Usually seen in childhood (poor growth, failure to gain weight).

Treatment and prevention: Need a gluten-free diet. Avoid cereal wheat, rye, barley and possibly oats. Reintroduction of gluten will lead to reoccurrence of symptoms. Maintenance to strict diet is essential.

Hepatitis B: Hepatitis B is a virus which can cause inflammation of the liver. A high frequency of chronic carriers (people with the virus but showing no symptoms) have been found in institutions for people with learning disability. Males are more infective than females. Transmission appears to occur through skin or by contact of the inside of the mouth with blood and other body fluids. The greatest risk of transmission is through people who are aggressive with biting and scratching behaviours.

Symptoms and signs: Often none. If present can include jaundice (yellow discolourization of the skin due to liver disease), nausea, loss of appetite, tenderness in right upper part of abdomen, and muscle aches.

Investigations: Blood test for antibodies (proteins produced by the body's immune system which help to neutralise infecting agents) to virus, liver function tests to assess status of liver. Will need to test other contacts.

Complications: Occasionally can result in liver failure or cause death.

Treatment and prevention: Good hygiene and Hepatitis B vaccination is important to reduce infection. During the acute phase bed rest and a nourishing diet is recommended.

Irritable Bowel Syndrome: Intermittent pain and irregular bowel habit. Often repeated episodes.

Causes: No one cause but reported to be associated with emotional distress.

Symptoms and signs: Pain in the lower left abdomen which is relieved by opening bowels. Alternating constipation and diarrhoea. Abdominal distention, wind. A long history of such problems is usually reported.

Investigations: Rarely needed but can screen for a serious medical problem (see constipation and diarrhoea above). Tests usually all normal.

Complications: Secondary emotional distress.

Treatment and Prevention: Reassurance and high-fibre diet can benefit the majority of people. Anti-diarrhoea drugs can be prescribed.

Chapter 11

GENITOURINARY SYSTEM

The quality of genitourinary care for people with learning disability (especially for women) remains poor. Little routine screening and health promotion takes place. Carers and families have to actively seek good counselling and guidance on menstrual, sexual and contraceptive issues (chapter 4). With appropriate teaching and support, many young women with Down syndrome could become responsible for their own needs. **As for other problems, the opinion of a doctor should be sought if the person themselves, families or carers have concerns.**

Gynaecological/Genital Issues: Many 'women's problems' require a high degree of sensitivity, not least on performing pelvic examinations. The insertion of a speculum may not be possible and sedation or external ultrasonography (procedure where sound waves are used to produce images on a screen) may be necessary. Whether adolescent girls with Down syndrome should be seen routinely for a pelvic examination remains controversial. Certainly early onset of periods (before age 10 years) or delayed periods (after age 18 years), irregular or heavy bleeding, painful periods, premenstrual tension should lead to a medical assessment. Prior to the examination counselling and education will need to be given and a number of visits may need to be made prior to a successful examination. Prescribing of medication for gynaecological reasons must consider other health problems such as epilepsy and diabetes. Most young females with Down syndrome develop periods at the same age as girls without learning disability (age of onset 10–14 years). The majority have normal regular periods but a significant number may have some problems. Menopause is reported to occur earlier in women with Down syndrome as compared to the general female population.

Problems present at birth in males and females with Down syndrome are not uncommon and may persist into adulthood:

Males

Hypospadias: Opening of the urethra on the underside of the penis. The penis may also curve downwards.
Cause: Present at birth.
Symptoms and signs: Problems can occur on passing urine. Achieving an erection may be difficult.
Investigations/Complications: Usually none.
Treatment: If causing concern a surgical correction procedure can take place (usually however this is done as an infant).

Phimosis: A condition where the foreskin of the penis is tight and there is difficulty in drawing it back over the head of the penis. Normal finding in infants.
Cause: Present at birth.
Symptoms and signs: There is difficulty in passing urine, ballooning out of foreskin on urination, difficulty in achieving a full erection.
Investigations: None usually required.
Complications: Occasionally an infection can occur.
Treatment: The problem can improve over time without medical intervention. Gently withdrawing the foreskin when in the bath (do not force) can be helpful for minor conditions. Severe cases may require a circumcision (removal of a part of the foreskin of the penis).

Undescended testis: Failure of the testis to be present in the scrotum usually affects one testis only but can affect both. Testes usually descend by 7 months of age.
Cause: Present at birth.

Investigations: None usually required.
Complications: Impaired sperm production and an increased risk of testicular cancer has been reported.
Treatment: Surgical intervention should be considered to lower the testis into the scrotum.

Females

Premenstrual syndrome (tension): Emotional and physical changes occurring one or two weeks before menstruation.
Cause: Unknown but probably related to hormonal changes associated with the normal menstrual cycle.
Symptoms and signs: Commonest symptoms include headaches, irritability, bloating, weight gain, breast tenderness, mood changes, fatigue, backache, lower abdominal pain and behavioural problems.
Investigations: For several consecutive months close monitoring of the menstrual cycle along with the emotional and behavioural changes.
Complications: May be associated with accident proneness. Can lead to a deterioration of epilepsy and lead to a mis-diagnosis of mood or behaviour changes.
Treatment and prevention: Understanding and sympathy are an important part of management. Use of a hot-water bottle, mild diuretics, analgesics, oral or long acting contraceptive, vitamin B6, primrose oil have been reported to have some beneficial effects. Severe depression can be treated with antidepressants.

Painful periods (dysmenorrhoea):
Cause: Usually related to hormonal changes. Can be associated with premenstrual tension. Late onset dysmenorrhoea can be due to an underlying medical cause (eg infection, hormonal imbalance).
Symptoms and signs: Cramp-like pain in the lower abdomen, backache, headache, nausea, vomiting, irritability, and behavioural problems can occur.
Investigations: Need to exclude a serious underlying cause by ultrasound examination (procedure using sound waves transmitted

to body to produce pictures) and/or by laparoscopy (examination of abdomen and pelvis directly by using flexible tube). A specialist assessment may be necessary.

Complications: Emotional distress. Secondary to cause.

Treatment and prevention: Mild painkillers (aspirin, naproxen), rest, and using a hot-water bottle can be beneficial. Anti-inflammatory medication such as Mefenamic Acid (Ponstan) can give some relief. If severe, ovulation can be stopped by use of the oral contraceptive pill.

Absence of menstrual periods (amenorrhoea): Condition where there are no periods before the age of 16 years or where periods which previously occurred now stop.

Causes: Many causes including delayed puberty, stress, pregnancy, menopause, hysterectomy, underlying medical cause eg hypothyroidism, adrenal gland disorder, ovary disorder, depression, drugs, anorexia, and the continuous use of the oral contraceptive pill. Often no underlying cause found.

Symptoms and signs: Absent periods. Other symptoms may be present due to the underlying cause.

Investigations: (See painful periods above). Can measure the level of the female sex hormones in blood.

Complications: Secondary to cause.

Treatment: Reassurance. Treat any underlying cause.

Irregular periods (oligomenorrhoea): Infrequent and unexpected periods.

Causes: Stress, the oral contraceptive pill. Menopause. Medical causes include thyroid disease, polycystic ovary syndrome, pelvic infection, side-effects of drugs. Often no cause can be found.

Symptoms and signs: Bleeding between periods, or whilst on the Pill.

Investigations/Complications: (see dysmenorrhoea above).

Treatment: Reassurance. Treat cause if known.

Heavy periods (menorrhagia):

Causes: Indicates hormonal imbalance, pelvic infection, thyroid disease, and stress. A cause may not be found.

Symptoms and signs: Difficult to assess accurately. Good indication is an increased use of tampons or sanitary pads.

Investigations: (See dysmenorrhoea above). A sample of tissue from the uterus by 'D and C' (dilation of the cervix and removal of material from the inner wall of the uterus) can help to determine cause.

Complications: Can develop anaemia.

Treatment: Treat underlying cause. Iron replacement for anaemia. The oral contraceptive pill or a hysterectomy can control or stop periods.

Endometriosis: Condition in which fragments of the lining of the uterus are found outside the womb.

Cause: Unknown.

Symptoms and signs: Sometimes none present. Commonly include abnormal or heavy periods, severe abdominal pain, diarrhoea or constipation.

Complications: Can cause cysts to form. Risk of infertility increased.

Investigations: A gynaecological assessment is needed. Laparoscopy (examination of the inside of the abdomen with a viewing instrument) will show lesions.

Treatment: Drugs can be given to stop periods. A hysterectomy can be considered.

Menopause: Cluster of symptoms around time of last period.

Cause: Natural and normal change in sexual hormones with age.

Symptoms and signs: Most women experience no other symptoms other than irregular and then stopping of periods. Other symptoms include fluid retention, palpitations, sweating and feeling hot, headaches, breast discomfort, changes in behaviour or mood.

Complications: Increased risk of osteoporosis (bone loss).

Investigations: Usually none required but exclude thyroid or psychological condition.

Treatment: Reassurance and explanation, hormone replacement therapy (HRT) may be given.

Urinary issues: Several problems of the urinary system are found in adults with Down syndrome. Many of these will be present since birth. These include a reduced weight and size of the kidneys, dilatation and obstruction of the kidney vessels and simple kidney cysts. Presence of structural abnormalities at any site of the urinary system (Figure 9) will increase susceptibility to impaired kidney function and increase the risk of infections.

Figure 9: Structures of the Urinary System

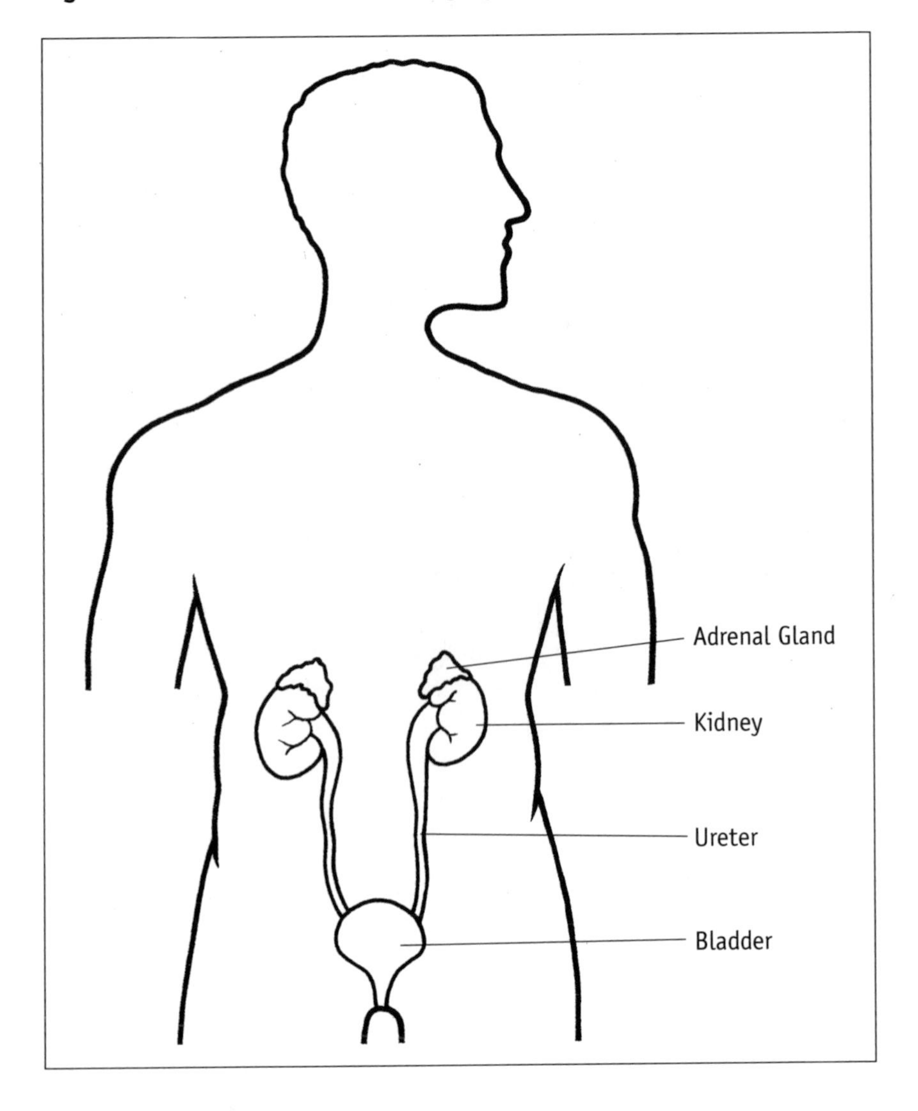

Urinary tract infection:

Causes: The majority of infections have no identifiable cause, are single attacks and do not cause any significant damage. When the cause is known it is usually due to bacteria from the person's own bowel area. Factors include poor personal hygiene, chemicals in bath water, wearing of nappies or sanitary towels and use of a urinary catheter. Less common but more important causes include abnormalities present at birth, kidney stones and a bladder obstruction. Recurrent attacks can occur.

Symptoms and signs: Usually there is an increased frequency of passing urine by day and night, pain on passing urine, abdominal pain and tenderness, blood in urine, urge to pass urine and smelly urine. These symptoms suggest a lower tract infection or 'cystitis', but an infection of the kidneys can cause loin pain and tenderness usually with a fever. Occasionally infections can present with no symptoms. Behavioural and/or emotional deterioration can be caused by a urinary tract infection.

Complications: The important complications include spread of the infection into the blood stream (septicaemia), shock or a scarring anywhere along the urinary system.

Investigations: Involve trying to detect the type of infection and whether any damage has been caused. Tests include an analysis of a mid-stream specimen of urine for bacteria, cystoscopy (tube passed into the bladder), ultrasound scanning (procedure where sound waves are used to produce pictures) and an abdominal x-ray examination.

Treatment: A high fluid intake and regular emptying of the bladder can help to flush out any bacteria. A potassium citrate mixture and/or antibiotics may be prescribed. Patients who are acutely ill may require admission to hospital. For individuals with recurrent infections a search should be made for a cause eg stones, birth abnormalities in the structure of the urinary system.

Urinary tract obstruction: This can occur anywhere between the kidney and urethral outlet, leading to dilatation of the tract above the obstruction and impaired kidney function.

Causes: Include those inside the tract eg stones, blood clot, rarely a tumour; a problem within the wall of the tract eg muscle dysfunction, stricture, pin-hole outlet, or outside the tract eg an enlarged prostate.

Symptoms and signs: Include loin pain, inability to urinate or reduced urine output, infection, difficulty in passing urine, a need to pass urine often, and incontinence. Can cause severe distress, behavioural and emotional deterioration.

Investigations: Blood tests especially for urea and creatinine levels (measures of kidney function). Detect site and cause of obstruction by ulirasonography (procedure using sound waves to produce pictures) and by x-ray examination of the urinary system.

Complications: If untreated can lead to kidney failure (below).

Treatment: Need to relieve any obstruction and treat any underlying cause, this may require surgical intervention. Treat any associated infection.

Kidney failure: An inability of the kidneys to excrete bodily waste products. Can be sudden (acute) or gradual (chronic).

Causes: a) Acute kidney failure may be due to a range of causes which include pre-kidney problems (eg hypotension, blood infection), kidney problems (eg infection) and post-kidney problems (eg urinary tract obstruction). b) Common causes of chronic kidney failure include kidney inflammation, infection, diabetes, hypertension, long-standing urinary tract obstruction.

Symptoms and signs: Include malaise, anorexia, decreased or increased urine output, nausea and vomiting, water retention, breathlessness, anaemia, and hypertension. Behavioural and/or emotional deterioration can occur.

Investigations: Need to monitor severity and any deterioration in kidney function. Regular examination of the urine and blood biochemistry (particularly for urea and creatinine-measures of kidney function) is necessary. Ultrasound (sound waves transmitted to body and reflected back to produce images), x-ray examination or a small sample of kidney tissue (kidney biopsy) may be undertaken. Regular blood pressure measurements necessary to detect hypertension.

Complications: If kidney failure is not treated an imbalance of the body's blood chemistry will result and can lead to death.

Treatment: Acute kidney failure is a medical emergency and requires immediate hospital management eg replace lost fluid, surgically remove obstruction. In chronic kidney failure underlying causes should be treated. Blood pressure control, dietary advice, use of diuretics and steroids are important to good management. If there is severe kidney failure, haemodialysis (removal of toxins from the blood by means of being attached to a specially designed machine) or a kidney transplant should be considered.

Prostate enlargement: The prostate gland is a gland found in men around the urinary tract. A significant enlargement occurs in older men.

Causes: Usually related to age but occasionally can be due to cancer.

Symptoms and signs: Frequent urination, waking at night to go to the toilet, delay in initiating urination, reduced force, and dribbling are frequent symptoms.

Investigations: A manual examination of the prostate can often detect an enlarged gland. X-ray examination, cystourethroscopy (passing of flexible tube through urethra to visualise the lower urinary system) and/or scans can be performed to confirm any enlargement, the reason for enlargement and any effects due to the swelling. Urine examination and blood tests (urea and creatinine levels) should be undertaken to assess kidney function. Can have a blood test to detect a marker for prostate cancer.

Complications: An obstruction of the bladder outflow can lead to bladder distension. Can occasionally lead to kidney failure (above).

Treatment: If the enlargement is mild it can be treated with drugs. A significant enlarged prostate will require surgery intervention (transurethral resection). If cancer is present surgical removal of the prostate and radiotherapy is required.

Chapter 12

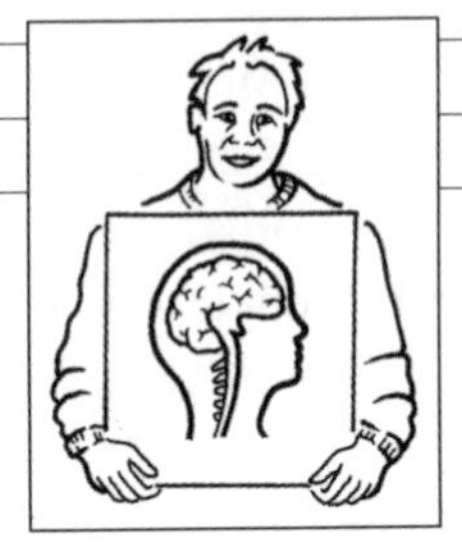

NERVOUS SYSTEM

The nervous system consists of the brain, the spinal cord and numerous smaller nerves which are widespread over the body. The nervous system interacts with virtually all other systems in the body and therefore has a significant role to play in the health status of a person. Detailed information from the person with Down syndrome and from their carers is most important to find the site and cause of any problem. **Medical attention should always be sought for any condition giving cause for concern.**

Headache: Produced by stimulation of pain-sensitive structures within the skull or tissue around the skull.

Causes: Single episode: Common, and can vary from a minor complaint to a serious acute emergency. Attention needs to be paid to the site, the suddenness of onset, and to any associated fever or rash. A severe single episode of a headache may be due to an apparent cause such as toothache or following head trauma. Less obvious but more serious causes can be due to life-threatening conditions such as meningitis. *Recurrent headaches:* May be due to recurrent ear infections (chapter 7), impaired visual acuity (sharpness of vision), sinusitis, glaucoma (chapter 6), migraine, or tension headaches.

Symptoms and signs: Tension headaches and headaches due to eyestrain usually present as 'a tight band' around the head, pressure behind the eyes, throbbing or with a bursting sensation. Migraine attacks can present with features prior to the headache of visual symptoms, speech difficulties, nausea, vomiting or irritability. Symptoms of an underlying cause may be present eg tender cheekbones in sinusitis.

Investigations: Often not necessary but depends on the cause. Can include blood tests, skull x-ray (when a head injury has occurred), brain scan and a lumbar puncture (procedure to take fluid from around the spine from the lower back).

Complications: Most headaches are self-limiting. Complications can follow meningitis or a brain haemorrhage.

Treatment and prevention: Depends on the type of headache. Tension headaches can benefit from reassurance, avoiding cause, analgesia, physical treatment (massage, relaxation), increased fluid intake, sleep and from a course of antidepressants (drugs used to treat depression). Migraine headaches can benefit from reassurance, avoiding dietary triggering foods, paracetamol and prophylactic medication to prevent migraine. **Following serious head trauma, or if with a headache there is associated vomiting, disturbed consciousness or visual loss a medical assessment is recommended.**

Unconsciousness: Altered state of alertness.

Causes: Concussion is a brief loss of consciousness due to a head injury eg owing to a fall, traffic accident. Usually there is no associated damage but the person should be observed closely and the doctor informed. *Fainting* is a temporary loss of consciousness due to poor oxygen supply to the brain. Can be due to pain, stress, shock, fear, prolonged coughing or straining, low blood pressure, medication, heart disease, hypothyroidism or diabetes (chapter 15). *Coma* is a loss of consciousness with lack of response to stimuli eg pinching or shouting. A coma is usually due to a more serious condition including severe head injury, seizures, build up of poisons (eg drugs, liver or kidney failure), diabetes, brain infection or meningitis. After a seizure, loss of consciousness is common and can last from a few minutes to several hours.

Investigations: Need to determine severity and cause. Tests can include blood and urine analysis for diabetes, hormones and major organ function. More detailed tests include electroencephalography (EEG, investigation of the brain function by measurement of electrical brain activity), a brain scan and a lumbar puncture (procedure to take fluid from around the spine from the lower back).

Complications: Depends on the cause, but if medical treatment is not obtained can prove to be fatal.

Treatment: Concussion: Rest for 24 hours under supervision is usually adequate. **If there is disturbed breathing, vomiting, problems with vision then see doctor for further assessment.** *Fainting:* The person should sit down and lean forward, head down between knees or alternatively lie down and raise legs. **If unconscious for several minutes seek medical help.** *Seizure:* (see below). After the immediate management a further detailed medical assessment will be required. Information regarding diabetic status, epilepsy, medication, trauma is essential. *Coma:* Check breathing, check airways are clear. **If not breathing start artificial respiration.** If the person is breathing normally place them into the 'recovery position' as follows:

(a) lying on their back turn the person's head onto their left side
(b) put left arm by their side and slide it under their buttock
(c) lay right arm across chest and cross right leg over left leg
(d) from the left side, lean over and grasp clothes at hip and pull person over onto their left side
(e) bend right arm and right leg to give support, free left arm and keep head tilted back and airway clear.
(f) seek help, do not leave the person alone and no food or drink should be given.

Epilepsy (seizures): A nervous condition characterised by a convulsive attack and change in consciousness.

Cause: Changes in the electrical discharge in the brain can lead to an altered level of consciousness and abnormal movements (a seizure). *Single seizure:* Can be triggered by a fever, infections, drugs, physical illness, heart disease. *Recurrent seizures:* Overall probably more common in people with Down syndrome than in the general population. There appears to be three age peaks, in infants, young adults and the older population. For the older population tonic-clonic and myoclonic seizures are common (often associated with Alzheimer's disease – chapter 16).

Seizure types:

a) Generalised (whole of brain affected and consciousness lost). Tonic-clonic: person loses consciousness, stiffens, falls and limbs jerk. Myoclonic: uncontrollable jerks. Atonic: a loss of muscle tone and the person falls down. Absences: temporally unresponsive, staring. No falling but there may be associated jerking of an arm. Cannot be interrupted by talking or touching. Usually last 10 seconds but several seizures can occur each day.

b) Partial seizures (only a limited part of the brain is affected. Localised unusual symptoms eg tingling, flashing lights can occur). Simple partial seizure – symptoms of a partial seizure but person remains conscious. Complex partial seizure – symptoms of a partial seizure but there is a loss of awareness.

c) Secondary generalised seizures. A partial seizure (above) spreads to involve the whole of the brain and there are features also of a generalised seizure.

Investigations: A detailed history of the seizure is important. Videotaping of episodes can be extremely useful. Other tests include an electrogram (EEG – recording of the electrical brain pattern), brain scan, blood screen and blood anticonvulsant drug levels.

Complications: Injury, choking, behaviour and emotional changes are common. Status epilepticus (repeated seizures without full recovery between fits) is a serious complication. Epilepsy can lead to death if severe complications occur or if seizures are severe or prolonged.

Treatment and prevention: First aid: Cushion head with hands if nothing else available. Do not physically restrain or move during seizure. Do not place anything in the mouth. Loosen tight clothing. When the attack has finished place the person on their side in the recovery position (for details see above). Do not leave the person until fully recovered. **For prolonged seizures call ambulance or medical help.** Long-term treatment will involve taking of anti-convulsant drugs (group of drugs used to treat epilepsy eg diazepam, carbamazepine, sodium valproate) either to stop a fit or to try to prevent future seizures. Change in diet or psychological support can also be of benefit. The regular recording of seizure frequency is important. An identification card, education for family and carers on how to manage seizures can aid management. Regular medical reviews of drug therapy is necessary to prevent toxicity, reduce side effects and stop drug interactions.

Myoclonus: Sudden jerking of muscle or group of muscles.

Cause: Can occur in healthy people but seen commonly in adults with Down syndrome as part of a seizure or as part of Alzheimer's disease (chapter 16).

Symptoms and Signs: Sudden involuntary jerking of usually an arm or a leg. Night-time jerks are common and do not suggest any serious problem.

Investigations: Exclude epilepsy or underlying Alzheimer's disease.

Complications: Often none. Can occasionally trigger a generalised convulsion (see epilepsy above).

Treatment and prevention: Reassurance may be all that is necessary. Anticonvulsant medication will be prescribed if due to a seizure disorder.

Chapter 13

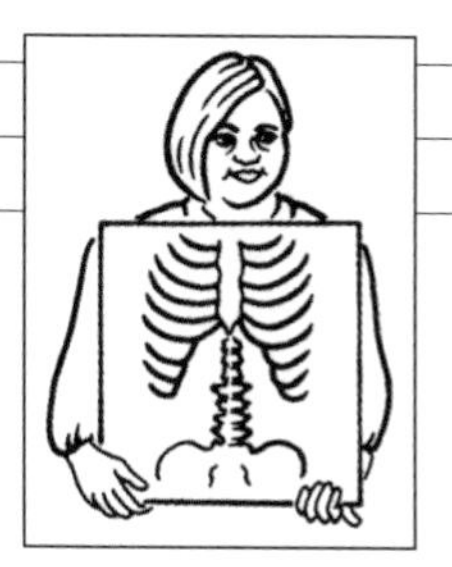

SKELETON, JOINTS AND DENTAL CARE

Skeletal and joint problems are common in adults with Down syndrome because of the differences in bone and tissue structure and because of the reduced muscle tone. The majority of problems can be attributed to the 'looseness' of ligaments secondary to changes in collagen (the building block of ligaments and muscles).

Teeth are important in the preparation of food for swallowing and digestion, in the production of speech and also in the appearance of the individual. The latter point may seem somewhat superfluous, perhaps even frivolous, but it is neither of these since appearance has a great deal to do with socialisation and social acceptability. Due to structural changes in the oral cavity, dry mouth (with more viscous saliva), delayed tooth eruption and missing permanent teeth, adults with Down syndrome are prone to experience more dental problems than average. Good oral cleanliness is essential and regular dental assessments by a dentist are important to prevent serious health problems because of the heart conditions commonly associated with Down syndrome.

It is a good idea to introduce people with Down syndrome to the feeling of having their teeth cleaned from as early as an age as possible. If the act of brushing can be accompanied with a simple song and can be turned into a game, the activity will come to be associated with a pleasurable experience and not develop into a debilitating struggle. Adults with Down syndrome generally want to take control of many activities themselves, and this includes teeth brushing. Whilst this is a very good thing in the long run, it is essential that they should be closely supervised. If the habit of effective teeth brushing is developed and maintained it will go a long way to ensuring that dental problems are minimised. **Annual check-ups should take place by a dentist who has experience in looking after people with learning disability.**

Skeleton and joints

Dislocation of Joints: This is the displacement of two bones in a joint. Commonly dislocated joints are the knee, hip, elbow, patella and thumb.

Causes: Due to 'loose' ligaments and reduced muscle tone.

Symptoms and signs: Include pain, loss of movement, joint looks misshapen, swelling, unable to weight bear, abnormal walking stance, distress and disturbed behaviour.

Investigations: An x-ray of the joint will show any abnormality present.

Complications: Nerve damage and paralysis is uncommon but can occur. Repeated dislocations can lead to degeneration of the joint.

Treatment and prevention: Minor dislocations may manipulate back by themselves. For others a splint may be needed to stop further movement and secondary damage, until manipulated back by a doctor. No eating or drinking before treatment as general anaesthesia may be given. For joints with repeated dislocations surgical intervention may be necessary to stabilise joint. Improved muscle mass can increase stability of joints. Care should be taken when undertaking physical activities to prevent reoccurrence of the dislocation.

Painful joints:

Causes: A long history would suggest arthritis (see osteoarthritis, rheumatoid arthritis below), but a short sudden onset may suggest trauma, gout, septic arthritis. Pain in the arm can be due to a neck problem or a painful knee due to a hip problem.

Symptoms and signs: Painful joint, stiffness, swelling, tenderness, loss of function, behaviour and emotional deterioration.

Investigations: Blood tests for evidence of inflammation, for presence of joint antibodies (proteins produced by the body against parts of the joint) and uric acid levels to rule out gout. X-ray examination or scan of the joint, joint aspiration (small amount of fluid in joint removed by insertion of needle) may be necessary.

Complications: Immobility and chronic problems can occur, if other problems are related to the underlying cause.

Treatment: Main treatment involves rest, lose weight, use of painkillers (non-steroidal anti-inflammatory drugs eg aspirin), steroid-based drugs, physical therapy (heat, hydrotherapy), and physiotherapy. Occasionally surgery (joint replacement) is necessary if problems persist.

Atlanto-occipital instability (AOI) and atlanto-axial instability (AAI): Joints at the top of the spine and at the base of the skull allow normal nodding and shaking movements of the head (Figure 10). In individuals with Down syndrome these joints can be more lax and weaker than other joints, leading to damage to nearby nerves. Atlanto-axial instability (AAI) is more common than AOI.

Cause: Laxity of ligaments and joints.

Symptoms and signs: Usually none but can result in spinal nerves being trapped. Symptoms of spinal cord involvement are weakness in arms and/or legs, problems in walking, local neck pain and discomfort, neck stiffness, head tilt, urinary incontinence, and brisk tendon reflexes especially of the ankles. Symptoms can occur following injury and can be quite sudden.

Investigations: X-ray or scan of the upper spine.

Complications: Dislocation of the AOI or AAI joints can lead to serious spinal cord damage.

Treatment and prevention: If AOI or AAI is present, then need to consider exclusion from sport activities eg gymnastics, diving, butterfly stroke in swimming, football, trampolining. Caution is required with over extension of neck (eg when having a general anaesthestic). Head rests are useful when travelling to prevent whiplash injuries. Surgical intervention may be necessary to stabilize joint if AAI or AOl is present and leading to nerve damage. This involves fusion with bone grafts or metal wire for affected joint. Screening for AOI and AAI by routine cervical x-

Figure 10: Upper Spine

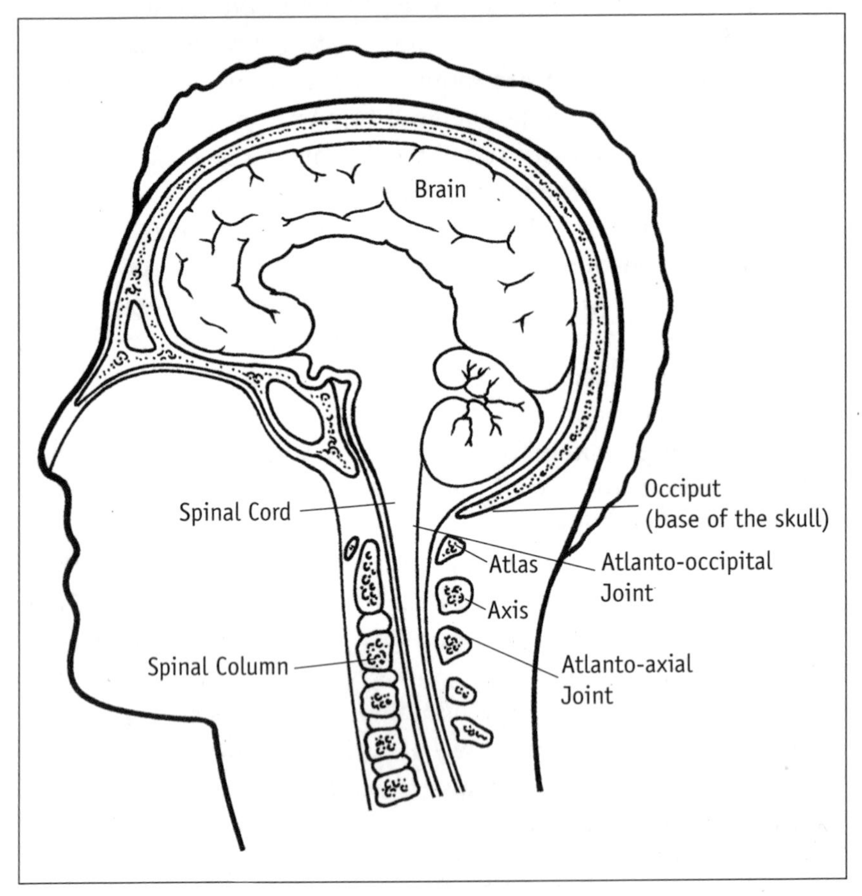

rays is no longer recommended and is unlikely to be helpful in deciding which individuals may be at risk of nerve involvement. **Medical opinion should be sought if any symptoms suggestive of cervical spine problems occur.**

Feet Problems: Include flat feet, dry feet, fissures, split nails, callosities, infection of toe-nails, wide-based walking stance and external rotation of foot.

Causes: Minor deformities are extremely common due to looseness of ligaments, obesity and ill-fitting shoes.

Symptoms and signs: Commonly include abnormal appearance, pain in foot, abnormal walking posture, and ingrowing toe-nails.

Treatment and prevention: An assessment by a foot specialist (podiatrist) may be necessary. Depends on the cause but foot exercises (eg walking on tip-toes), shoe inserts, specifically designed shoes can prevent some problems. Surgical correction of deformities is occasionally required. Medication can be given for infections. Psychological intervention may be necessary to get the person to have their toe-nails cut without a struggle.

Scoliosis: Side to side curvature of the spine, usually middle of the back.
Causes: Present at birth, laxity of ligaments, poor posture.
Symptoms: Spinal deformity, odd postures, abnormal walking.
Investigations: A spinal x-ray will show the deformity.
Complications: If minor change is present usually no associated problems. If severe can lead to breathing problems, heart problems, chest discomfort and problems with balance and walking.
Treatment: If minor no intervention is necessary other than to monitor severity. If severe, may need surgical intervention with spinal fusion of vertebrae to straighten spine.

Osteoarthritis: 'Wear and tear' inflammation and degeneration of a joint. Affects mainly large joints and cervical spine.
Causes: Associated with increasing age, obesity and immobility.
Symptoms: (See painful joint above).
Investigations: X-ray or scan of joint, blood tests for evidence of joint inflammation.
Complications: Can lead to degeneration of the joint, nerves can become trapped.
Treatment: (See painful joint above).

Rheumatoid Arthritis: An inflammation of several and usually symmetrical joints.
Causes: Possible autoimmune condition where the body's own defence mechanism attacks its own joints.
Symptoms and signs: Include a gradual onset of joint pain (usually hands or feet), stiffness, tenderness, swelling, reduced function, and deformity. Joints on either side of the body are affected at the same time.

Investigations: Elevated measures of joint inflammation in blood and evidence of abnormal defence response. Test for specific marker for rheumatoid arthritis called 'rheumatoid factor'. An x-ray of the joints can show damage caused.

Complications: Uncommon, but loss of function of joints, nerve compression (eg cervical spine involvement) or an inflammation of some other body organ can occur.

Treatment: (See painful joint above).

Teeth

Toothache:

Causes: Common conditions include tooth decay, eruption of wisdom teeth, mouth ulcers, gum disease, pain from sinuses or from ears.

Symptoms and signs: In tooth decay there is initially a sharp but short-lived pain. Later severe and longer lasting pain occurs. Toothache pain is worst on eating or drinking. Person may also suffer from jaw ache, swollen face, loss of appetite, distress, emotional or behavioural problems (hand-flapping, shouting, head-banging, biting). Putting a hand to the face or a finger in mouth is a common feature. The site of the toothache will have a tender tooth.

Investigations: Dental assessment. X-ray of teeth.

Complications: Usually none but the serious condition of bacterial endocarditis (chapter 8) must be prevented.

Treatment: Painkillers (paracetamol), heat to side of face and use of gel may give temporary relief. Need to treat underlying cause.

Prevention of teeth disease: Good dental care involves a number of issues: daily brushing of teeth and gums, regular check-ups, early treatment for problems, correct tooth brushing and a good diet to reduce sugar. Use of floss and fluoride therapy is essential to prevent decay. Encourage eating of fruit and vegetables rather than sweets and soft drinks, and encourage use of mouthwashes and mouth rinses. Need to regularly remove scales and plaque. Disclosing tablets (food dye) may be used to disclose the plaque on teeth as an aid to thorough cleaning. **The presence of heart disease or other health problems needs to be mentioned to the dentist. Antibiotics will need to be given prior to dental treatment if a heart lesion is present.** Time should be spent in finding a good dentist experienced with working with people with Down syndrome.

Tooth decay (Caries): Tooth decay occurs mainly in young adults. Decay of the tooth root (exposed by shrinking of the gums) can be a problem in older people.

Causes: Plaques form due to bacterial action on saliva and food particles. Sugar in food is fermented and acid is formed which destroys enamel and over time leads to tooth decay. Sources of sugar include sweets, honey, fizzy drinks, fruit juices, fruit cordials, biscuits, cakes, frosted cereals, canned fruit, baked beans and salad cream.

Symptoms and signs/Investigations/Complications: (See toothache above). In the early stages there may be no pain.

Treatment and prevention: Best to avoid sugary foods, especially as snacks between meals and just before going to bed. Brushing teeth with fluoride toothpaste makes outer covering of teeth (enamel) more resistant to bacterial action. Early stages of tooth decay may be helped by the application of a fluoride varnish. In severe cases the decayed area will need to be removed and replaced with a filling and/or root canal treatment. May need to extract tooth.

Improper fitting together of upper and lower teeth (Malocclusions):

Causes: Missing teeth, small teeth, peg-shaped teeth are common findings.

Symptoms and signs: Poorly spaced teeth, lower jaw too far back or too far forward leading to over-biting.

Investigation: Dental assessment.

Complications: There is an increased risk of tooth decay and gum disease.

Treatment: If severe, correct by use of braces and/or extraction of teeth.

Inflammation of the gums (Gingivitis): Common, often affecting lower jaw front teeth and upper jaw back teeth.

Causes: Often due to poor dental hygiene. Toxins produced by bacteria in dental plaque can irritate the gums and they become inflamed.

Symptoms and signs: (See toothache above), tender and swollen gums, gums bleed easily, bad breath. May avoid brushing teeth.

Investigation: Dental assessment.

Complications: Loss of teeth, formation of cysts (collections of fluids) or abscesses (collections of pus) can result.

Treatment: (See toothache above). If bleeding is noted during brushing, spend a little more time on the affected area. With careful and thorough removal of dental plaque the condition should resolve in about two weeks. If bleeding persists see dentist. Use of a gel containing chlorhexidine (Corsodyl) may help.

Inflammation of gums around teeth (Periodontitis):

Causes: Toxins produced by plaque can damage the periodontal area and cause bone around the tooth to be lost. Periodontitis generally follows on as a natural progression from untreated gingivitis (above).

Symptoms and signs: In the early stages this condition is superficially indistinguishable from gingivitis (above). Over a period of time the tooth appears to become longer as the gums recede and as the root of the tooth is exposed, pain may be experienced when it is stimulated mechanically (tooth brushing), chemically (sugary foods) or thermally (hot or cold food). Halitosis (bad breath) is a common feature of periodontal disease. As bone is progressively destroyed the tooth becomes noticeably loose within the socket. Eventually so much of the support tissues are lost that chewing on the affected tooth/teeth becomes painful as the load exceeds their capacity to bear it. At this stage hard food will be avoided in preference for soft. However, the affected tooth will often appear to be quite sound and undecayed. It is not unusual to find that the roots of the teeth in people with Down syndrome are shorter than usual. This can result in teeth becoming loose sooner than might otherwise be expected.

Complications: Periodontal abscesses (collections of pus) may develop. These bear a superficial resemblance to abscesses produced by tooth decay, being extremely painful and producing similar swellings.

Investigations: Dental assessment.

Treatment and prevention: (See gingivitis above).

Grinding of teeth (Bruxism):

Causes: Often no specific cause found. Known causes include anxiety, dental malocclusions (above), and reduced facial muscle tone.

Symptoms and signs: Rhythmic grinding or clenching usually during sleep but daytime also.

Complications: Commonly include wearing away of teeth, loosening of teeth, and stiffness of jaw.

Treatment: Regular monitoring for complications. A biteplate may give some relief.

Chapter 14

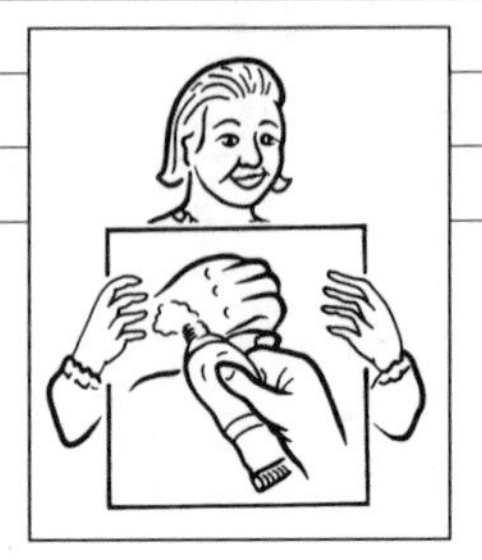

SKIN CONDITIONS

Skin, nail and hair problems may appear to be relatively minor in nature but such problems can cause considerable unrecognised distress to individuals and to their family and carers.

Spots (Acne): Very common. Spots often occur in areas of the face, back and chest. Usually begin in puberty. They are thought to be affected by the levels of sex hormones.
Causes: Blockage of hair/sweat ducts leading to build-up of secretions.
Symptoms and signs: 'Blackheads', 'whiteheads', cysts, boils, pimples. Spots can heal whilst others appear.
Investigations: If severe need to exclude an imbalance of sex hormones.
Complications: Picking or squeezing of spots can lead to scarring. Social embarrassment.
Treatment and prevention: Several treatments have been proposed but all have limited benefit. These include a change in diet, frequent washing, sunshine/ultra-violet light, antibiotics, particular drugs for acne (called abrasives) and prescribing of the oral contraceptive pill. Usually acne settles over time.

Boils: An inflamed pus-filled area of skin. Usually on back, neck or groin.
Causes: Bacterial infection of the hair follicle.
Symptoms and signs: Painful, red, tender swelling. Swells with pus. Eventually heals to leave scar.

Investigations: Need to exclude diabetes. If recurrent boils occur may need to swab nose and armpits to detect a possible site harbouring bacteria.

Complications: Usually none.

Treatment and prevention: When a lesion develops will need to swab area with antiseptic and break the skin with sterile needle to release the pus. Antibiotics may be necessary. Recurrent boils will require more intensive therapy.

Eczema (Atopic dermatitis): A particular type of inflammation of the skin. More common in children. By teenage years the majority of people will be clear of the disease. Adult eczema usually involves back of neck, elbows, wrists, ankles and knees.

Causes: Often no known cause. Can be due to allergies eg food. Person may also have asthma or hay fever.

Symptoms and signs: Commonly very dry skin, red, scaly, weepy and oozing, itchy, discomfort, and excoriations. Can be exacerbated with heat, humidity, drying of skin, contact with clothes. Emotional and behavioural difficulties can occur.

Investigations: Usually none required.

Complications: Secondary infections, and thickening of skin can occur.

Treatment and prevention: Sympathetic explanation to person and carers. Can use emollients (agents which soften skin, for example E45 and unguentum merck) applied to damp skin after bathing. Need to have warm, not hot baths, and to avoid use of perfumed soaps and wool clothing. Pat dry, do not rub skin. Sunlight/ultraviolet light can help. Mild skin steroid creams (used sparingly and with caution), tar, antibiotics, anti-histamine drugs (for itching) can be given. Specialist care from a dermatologist may be required.

Psoriasis: A chronic skin disease with thickened patches of inflamed red skin. Fluctuating course.

Causes: Often no known cause. Can be associated with a throat infection and made worse with emotional upset and trauma.

Symptoms and signs: Redden silvery scaled plaques usually over elbows, knees, and scalp. Finger-nails can become thickened and pitted. Itching is less than with eczema. Often symmetrical lesions.

Investigations: Usually none required.

Complications: Joint, scalp, joints or nail involvement can occur.

Treatment and prevention: Emollient (substance to soften skin) cream, Dithranol and steroid cream for the skin are the main forms of treatment. Ultraviolet/sunbathing (with care) has been shown to be beneficial.

Seborrhoeic dermatitis: Inflammation of skin where there is a high area of sebaceous glands (glands of the body which produce oils). Usually on face, scalp, chest and back.

Causes: Unknown but made worse by stress.

Symptoms and signs: Include redness, pustules, scaly, itchy and rash.

Investigations: Usually none required.

Complications: Can spread to areas of face, eyebrows, nasal folds, ears.

Treatment and prevention: Avoid scratching and irritating substances. Shampoos with fungistatic action can be of initial help. Use 3–7 times per week. Antibiotic or steroid creams can also be beneficial.

Xerosis: Dry, pale skin with poor elasticity.

Cause: Unknown but more common with increasing age.

Symptoms and signs: Dry cracked skin, can be itchy and scaly.

Investigations/Complications: Usually none.

Treatment and prevention: Avoid drying soaps and oils to skin after bathing. Lubricating creams and creams to soften the skin may help.

Hair Loss (Alopecia):

Causes: Often no cause found. Possibly due to an autoimmune association (body defences attack itself), or premature ageing. Severe stress, hormonal imbalance, drugs and iron deficiency can be known causes.

Symptoms and signs: Patches of hair loss over any part of body but normally the scalp. Hair may regrow or develop into total hair loss (Alopecia totalis).

Investigations: Need to rule out underlying cause such as thyroid disease.

Complications: Emotional and social disability.

Treatment: Active treatment is possible but this will depend on the degree of concern caused to the person with Down syndrome and their carers by the hair loss. Small areas of hair loss can regrow without active treatment. Severe hair loss can be treated with medication under medical supervision. Large doses of steroids can improve regrowth but a relapse is likely after the treatment is stopped. Side-effects from the medication is an important concern eg weight gain, puffiness, reduced appetite. Other drugs, such as minoxidil have also been shown to be beneficial. Conservative management eg wearing of a wig is often appropriate and certainly much safer than active treatment.

Vitiligo: Areas of loss of pigmentation on skin.

Causes: Often no obvious cause. Occasionally due to thyroid disease, autoimmunity (body defences attack itself) or old injuries.

Symptoms and signs: Patches of well-defined areas of white skin. Can appear anywhere on body; commonly on the hands, elbows, feet and face.

Investigations: Exclude an underlying condition.

Complications: Affected areas susceptible to sunburn and therefore must be covered or sun creams used.

Treatment and prevention: May spontaneously improve. Steroid cream can be used with medical advice and caution. Particular forms of medication along with ultra-violet light may be considered.

Cheilitis: Fissuring and crusting of lips.

Causes: Often no cause found. Occasionally due to eczema, infections or nutritional deficiencies.

Symptoms and signs: Redness, scaling and itchiness around lips.

Investigations/Complications: Usually none required.

Treatment: Moisturisation of lips with eg white petroleum. Treat any underlying cause.

Cutis marmorata and acrocyanosis: Discolourization of skin. Common finding in adults with Down syndrome.

Causes: Nerves and smaller blood vessels become sensitive to cold temperature.

Symptoms and signs: Cutis marmorata is a bluish mottling of the skin. Acrocyanosis is a cold-red discolourization of the hands and feet.

Investigations: A medical assessment to exclude a serious blood circulation problem.

Treatment and prevention: Keep extremities warm with increased clothing and heating.

Tinea pedis (athlete's foot): Infection of the feet/toes.

Causes: Fungal infection.

Symptoms and signs: Scaling, cracking, itching, redness of toes. Blistering of feet can occur.

Investigations: Usually none required but can examine scrapings from feet for fungi.

Treatment: Foot powders with antifungal agent. Potassium permanganate foot soaks. Miconazole powder, oral griseofulvin to treat fungus.

Onychomycosis: Infection of finger and toe nails.

Causes: Fungal infection

Symptoms and signs: Nails become opaque, white, thickened, friable or brittle.

Investigations: If severe can take clippings for analysis for the fungus.

Treatment: Antifungal medication eg Griseofulvin usually prescribed. Therapy for several years may be required.

Chapter 15

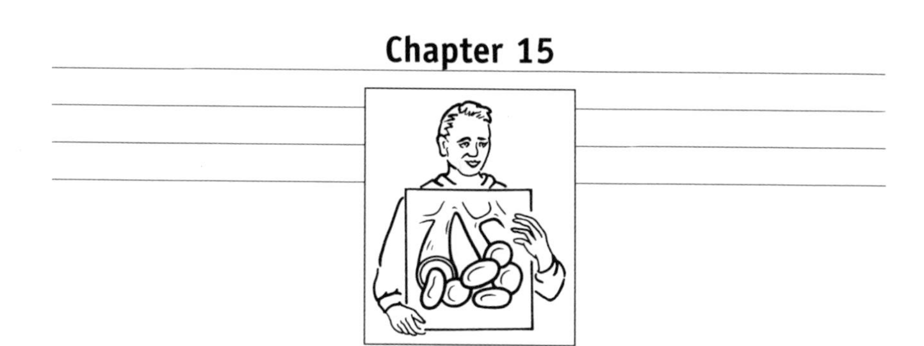

HORMONAL AND BLOOD-RELATED PROBLEMS

Hormones are chemicals produced by particular glands in the body specifically to have an effect on the function of one or more organs some distance away. The most important glands include the pituitary gland, the thyroid gland, adrenal glands, pancreas, ovaries (females) and testes (males) (Figure 11). Their action may be time-specific eg on sexual maturation and on growth, or may occur throughout life eg blood sugar control by insulin. The level of a hormone in the blood needs to be within certain limits, too much or too little can cause serious ill-health.

Blood contains a vast number of substances which play an important part in healthy bodily function. Such substances may be increased or decreased in quantity or be abnormal in shape or size. Regular screening of the levels of the blood substances is recommended for all persons with Down syndrome. A **medical opinion should be sought if carers have any concerns.**

A) Hormones

Thyroid disorders: The thyroid gland is found in the front part of the neck (Figure 11). It produces a number of hormones, in particular two called 'thyroxine' and 'tri-iodothyronine'. The gland is principally under the control of another hormone 'thyroid stimulating hormone' produced by the pituitary gland, a gland which serves to control and regulate many hormone producing

Figure 11: Glands of the Human Body

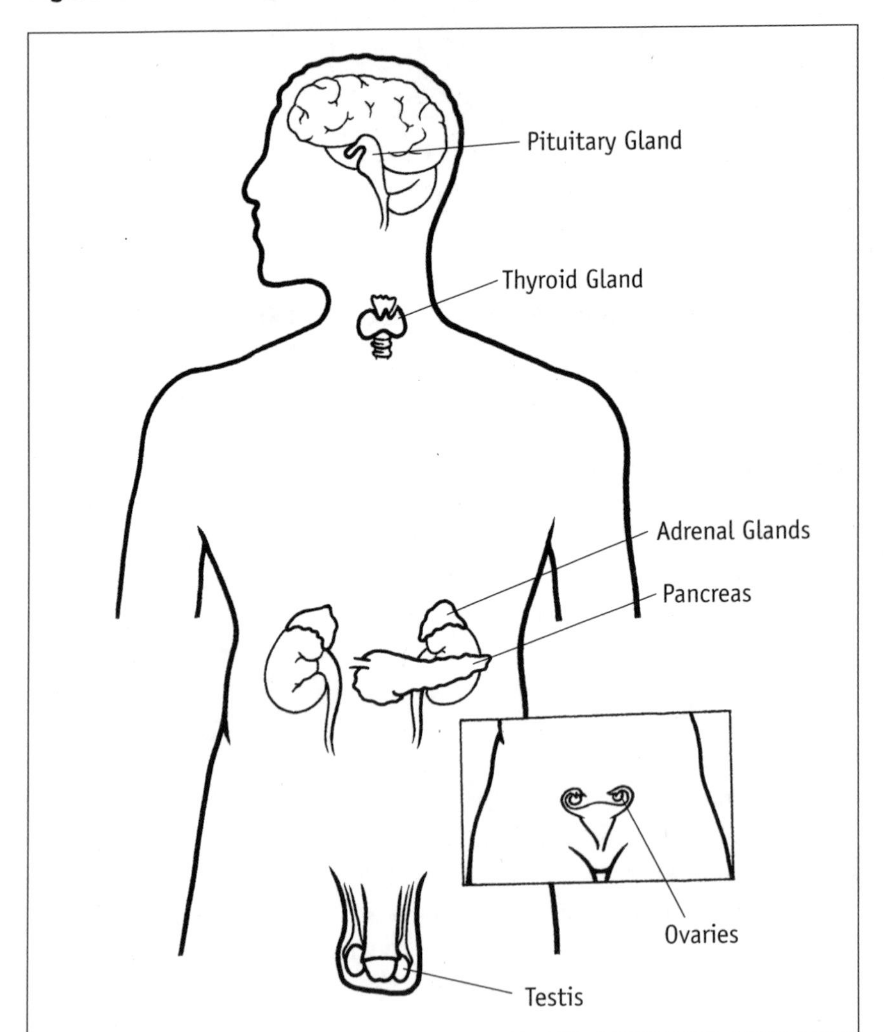

glands. The thyroid gland can become overactive (hyperthyroidism) and speed up the body's metabolism or become underactive (hypothyroidism) and slow down the body's metabolism. One-third of adults with Down syndrome have some evidence of a thyroid disorder.

Hypothyroidism: A condition where there is reduced activity of the thyroid gland. Associated low levels of the hormone thyroxine are found in the blood.

Causes: Can be present at birth. Birth hypothyroidism is uncommon and nowadays is detected by routine neonatal screening. Acquired hypothyroidism is the development of an underactivity of the thyroid gland during one's lifetime and is usually due to autoimmunity (the body's defence system attacks itself) or due to inflammation of the thyroid gland. The risk of developing hypothyroidism increases with age. Females are at a greater risk than males. Hypothyroidism can occasionally be due to medication (eg lithium) or following surgery on the thyroid gland.

Symptoms and signs: Many symptoms can occur. Slowing down, dry hair, weight gain, slow pulse, constipation, abnormal periods, mental deterioration, tiredness, heart failure, rough skin, loss of hair, deafness, anaemia, or early puberty.

Investigations: A diagnosis on appearance only can be difficult and blood tests are necessary. For hypothyroidism the blood level of the thyroid stimulating hormone is raised and the blood level of thyroxine is low. Antibodies (proteins produced by the body's immune system against the thyroid gland – see below) may be present.

Complications: Can cause premature puberty, heart disease (chapter 8) or present as a dementing illness (chapter 16).

Treatment and prevention: Thyroxine replacement therapy (a tablet a day) is necessary. The dose is increased depending on response and blood levels. Life-long therapy is often required. For borderline hypothyroidism (normal blood level of thyroxine but raised level of thyroid stimulating hormone) monitor if asymptomatic, if symptomatic or thyroid antibodies positive treat with thyroxine replacement. Routine screening recommended – minimum every 2 years.

Hyperthyroidism: An overactive thyroid gland. Increased blood levels of thyroxine. Less common than hypothyroidism.

Causes: Autoimmunity (the body's defence system attacks itself), inflammation of thyroid gland, drugs. Sometimes no cause found.

Symptoms and signs: Include weight loss, increased appetite, behavioural change, tremor, diarrhoea, irritability, swelling of the thyroid gland, breathlessness, thinning hair, heat intolerance, bulging eyes, and palpitations.

Investigations: Blood tests for thyroid hormone levels; low level of thyroid stimulating hormone but high blood level of thyroxine. High blood levels of thyroid stimulating hormone and thyroxine imply a problem with the pituitary gland. Thyroid antibodies (below) may be present.

Complications: Heart failure, behavioural or emotional problems.

Treatment: Need to reduce the thyroid gland activity by antithyroid drugs (carbimazole), surgery (thyroidectomy) or by giving radioactive iodine which reduces the function of the thyroid gland. An endocrinologist's (specialist doctor in the management of hormonal disorders) opinion is required. Hypothyroidism can develop after treatment.

Diabetes mellitus: A condition where there is a chronic high glucose level in the blood due to insulin deficiency or resistance to the action of insulin. Insulin dependent (condition requires insulin replacement therapy) and non-insulin dependent (condition can be controlled by strict diet and drugs) types. Insulin dependent type of diabetes usually affects younger people. Non-insulin dependent individuals are usually older and tend to be obese.

Causes: Often unknown. Autoimmune condition (the body's defence system attacks itself).

Symptoms and signs: Excessive urine output, thirst, weight change, skin infections, visual loss, confusion, loss of consciousness, behavioural problems.

Investigations: Need to test for a high blood glucose level (even after fasting), glucose and proteins in urine.

Complications: Includes 'hypoglycaemic attacks' of too little glucose in blood presenting with weakness, confusion, sweating, dizziness. High levels of glucose in blood can lead to 'diabetic ketoacidosis', a serious medical condition which presents with a 'fruity-smelling breath', loss of appetite, nausea, vomiting, stomach pains, coma. Long-term problems of diabetes include hypertension, poor circulation, heart disease, eye disease including cataracts, kidney damage, nerve damage and recurrent infections.

Treatment: Diet control and diabetic drugs can reduce blood glucose and be sufficient for most people. If this is unsuccessful insulin injections are required. Advice from a dietician and a specialist doctor in the treatment of diabetes is necessary. Need to measure diabetic control with urine tests for glucose and proteins, blood tests for glucose level and substance called 'glycosylated haemoglobin (HbA1)'. Careful monitoring and support is required to prevent serious complications. Advice and support to carers is important. **Immediate medical help must always be sought if severe complications occur.**

Gout: Metabolic disorder affecting joints.

Causes: Increased blood levels of uric acid leading to arthritis (usually in one joint). Big toe is most common joint affected, others include knee, ankle, wrist, and hands.

Symptoms and signs: Commonly the joint is red, swollen, tender, and very painful. Can have several attacks.

Investigations: Include a blood test to show a high blood uric acid, x-ray joint to show inflammation, removal of fluid from joint for uric acid crystals.

Complications: Arthritis in joint. Recurrent attacks not uncommon.

Treatment and prevention: Drink plenty of fluids. Non-steroidal anti-inflammatory drugs (aspirin, naproxen), or colchicine may be prescribed to reduce pain. Blood levels of uric acid can be lowered with other drugs (allopurinol or probenecid) which are given after the acute attack has settled. Need to avoid drinks with high uric acid levels.

Growth Hormone: This is a hormone which is produced by the pituitary gland that stimulates normal body growth. To assess growth correctly charts designed specifically for children with Down syndrome should be used. Children with Down syndrome may have an altered growth hormone metabolism and controversy surrounds the issue of whether children with Down syndrome may benefit from growth hormone replacement therapy. Adults are unlikely to benefit from growth hormone replacement (chapter 2).

Sex hormones: Few detailed studies have been reported. Generally for males the sex hormone testosterone is of a normal level. For females sex hormones may be at a normal level or increased (chapter 4).

B) Blood Diseases

A number of blood disorders are associated with Down syndrome although the underlying mechanisms for such findings remain unresolved. **Serious medical complications can result if not treated. A medical opinion should always be sought.**

Anaemia: A decrease in the level of haemoglobin in the blood.

Causes: Several causes. Iron deficiency (due to blood loss or insufficient intake of iron), vitamin B7 deficiency (if due to poor absorption in stomach called 'pernicious anaemia') folic acid deficiency, or bone marrow disease (see aplastic anaemia below).

Symptoms and signs: Usually fatigue, headaches, dizziness, fainting, breathlessness, pallor, and a fast heart rate. Heart failure, behavioural and emotional deterioration can occur.

Investigations: Need to measure the level of haemoglobin in the blood. If low, determine the type of anaemia and underlying cause. Blood tests can be undertaken to measure the level of important vitamins and minerals in the blood (Iron, B12, folic acid). If necessary may need to determine level of other blood cells, eg white cell count, platelets. If these are also abnormal will need to examine the production of these by the bone marrow (bone marrow aspiration – needle inserted into the bone and small amount of tissue removed).

Complications: Heart failure (chapter 8), can present as dementia (chapter 16).

Treatment and prevention: Depends on the underlying cause. Generally an increase in the dietary intake of iron (eg red meat) and vitamins will treat the anaemia. Iron tablets (ferrous sulphate), vitamin B_{12} injections can be prescribed if a change in the diet is not adequate. Rarely a blood transfusion is required.

Aplastic anaemia: Reduced number of red cells, white cells and platelets in blood.

Causes: Abnormality in the normal function of the bone marrow due to autoimmunity (condition where the body's own defence system attacks itself).

Symptoms and signs: (see anaemia above), increased risk of infections, bruising, and bleeding.

Investigations: Need to measure the level of the different cells in the blood. A bone marrow biopsy or a bone marrow aspiration (needle inserted into the bone and small amount of tissue removed) may be necessary.

Complications: Rarely leukaemia (below). Can if untreated lead to death.

Treatment: Will require blood transfusions, immuno suppression drugs (strong drugs which can reduce the body's immune function) and a bone marrow transplant may be necessary. Day-to-day care is required to treat any bleeding and infections which may occur.

Polycythemia: An increase in the blood concentration of haemoglobin, volume or number of red blood cells.

Causes: Often unknown. Can be present at birth or be due to heart disease (chapter 8).

Symptoms and signs: Can present with headaches, blurred vision, hypertension, tiredness, circulatory problems, gout.

Investigations: Blood tests for the haemoglobin level and the number of red blood cells in the blood is necessary. Need also to measure the size of the red blood cells and the thickness of the blood. A bone marrow aspiration (removal of a sample of the inner part of some bone marrow) is sometimes undertaken.

Complications: The development of a blood clot, a stroke or heart disease can occur.

Treatment: Need to remove cells from the blood by venesection (procedure where blood is taken from a vein – similar to a blood donation) to 'thin' the blood.

Neutropenia: Condition where there is a low blood count of some white cells called 'neutrophils'. Common finding in adults with

Down syndrome and usually indicates no serious underlying problem.

Causes: Unknown. Can be caused by drugs (eg chlorpromazine).

Symptoms and signs: Increased risk of infections.

Investigation: Usually none required. If severe then can measure the number of white blood cells in the blood and undertake a bone marrow aspiration (removal of a sample of the inner part of the bone with a needle) to detect any underlying disease present.

Complications: Secondary to any infection.

Treatment: Antibiotics when ill. Change medication if this is the cause.

Leukaemia: Cancer of the white blood cells. There are different types of leukaemias. Some can be of a short period but are often more aggressive (acute), others progress slowly and there is deterioration over several years (chronic). Common types include acute lymphoblastic leukaemia (ALL) and acute myeloid leukaemia (AML).

Causes: Unknown.

Symptoms and signs: Tiredness, fever, infections, pain in joints, bleeding, stomach pains, swollen abdomen, pallor, bruising, enlarged liver or spleen, swollen glands.

Investigations: Confirm the diagnosis by measuring the number of white blood cells in the blood and in the bone marrow by a bone marrow aspiration (needle inserted into the bone to obtain a piece of bone marrow). A lumber puncture (procedure where fluid is removed from the spine) may be undertaken to determine spread of disease.

Complications: Can lead to serious ill-health and in severe cases to death.

Treatment: Treatment from a specialist oncology (cancer) service is important. Blood transfusions (of red blood cells, platelets is necessary to maintain a high level of normal cells in blood), chemotherapy involving drugs and radiotherapy to kill cancer cells is usually necessary. There are a number of complications associated with these forms of therapy. These include a proneness to infections, a resultant high blood sugar level and ulcers in the mouth or in the bowel. There is a good outlook for ALL but less good for AML. Family support important. A bone marrow transplantation may be considered.

Myelofibrosis: An increased fibrosity of the bone marrow. Inability of the bone marrow to produce normal blood cells.
Causes: Unknown. Can be part of leukaemia.
Symptoms and signs/Investigations: (See anaemia above).
Complications: Recurrent infections, hypertension, blood clots, leukaemia. Can prove to be fatal.
Treatment: Blood transfusions are often required. Treat any underlying cause, treat infections.

Macrocytosis: An increase in the size of the red blood cells. Common abnormality in people with Down syndrome.
Causes: Usually no serious underlying cause. Often unknown. Known causes include vitamin B_{12} (folate) or thyroid deficiency. Possibly associated with Alzheimer's disease (chapter 16).
Symptoms and signs: Secondary to cause.
Investigations: Assess blood cell count and size of red blood cells, measure vitamin B_{12}, folic acid and thyroid hormone levels.
Complications: Secondary to cause.
Treatment: If there is no underlying cause which requires treatment just need to monitor on regular basis.

Transient myeloproliferative disorder: A condition similar to leukaemia but present for a brief time and not requiring treatment. However a proportion of those affected can develop leukaemia later on.

C) Immune system

The immune system protects the body from invading organisms such as bacteria and viruses. It does this by a number of means but primarily by producing antibodies (proteins produced by the body's immune system which help to neutralise infecting agents such as bacteria or viruses), and by activating white blood cells. Invaders are first recognized, then killed. Most importantly the makeup of the invader is remembered so that a further infection is readily dealt with. Some people with Down syndrome have a problem with their immune system leading to frequent and recurrent infections, cancers and the condition in which parts of their own body are attacked as if they were invaders (autoimmunity). Individuals prone to frequent recurrent infections can benefit from immunizations to influenza, pneumonia and Hepatitis B.

Several abnormalities in the immune system are seen in people with Down syndrome. The most common problems are reduction in some white cells (neutropenia) and an increase in autoimmunity (especially thyroid autoimunity). A high rate of Hepatitis B virus carriers has been reported (chapter 10).

Chapter 16

PSYCHOLOGICAL AND EMOTIONAL PROBLEMS

For adults with Down syndrome a wide range of psychological and emotional problems can occur. The 'Prince Charming' label often given to children with Down syndrome may distract from important behavioural and emotional problems which occur in adults and which require intervention. The accurate diagnosis of psychological and emotional problems is necessary for better physical and mental health. However, making the correct diagnosis is highly problematic because of the underlying cognitive impairments (particularly of communication), compounding medical conditions (eg sensory loss), poor test compliance and lack of knowledge regarding what is 'normal' and what is 'abnormal' for people with Down syndrome. **As for physical problems any concerns regarding emotional difficulties should lead to a medical opinion, where possible from an expert in the field of healthcare for adults with Down syndrome.**

Sleep disturbance: Common. May involve a problem in falling asleep, wakening during night, wakening early or sleeping at inappropriate times of the day.

Causes: May be due to no apparent reason. Can be part of a depression illness, anxiety disorder, physical condition, dementia, or due to side effects of medication.

Symptoms and signs: Problems with settling, waking at night, restless sleep, rituals, refusing to go to bed, snoring loudly.

Investigations: Need to rule out any underlying physical or psychological cause such as depression, anxiety, or sleep apnoea.

Complications: Include daytime behavioural problems, irritability, hyperactivity, and impaired daytime activities.

Treatment and prevention: Simple measures may help such as a routine sleep programme, relaxation, reduced caffeine intake, exercise, and a warm bath. A behavioural programme with minimal fuss, a set procedure at night with advice and support from a community nurse can be beneficial. Hypnotic medication can be given but is best avoided or used for a few days only.

Bereavement: A reaction in the months following death of someone close. Reaction varies from person to person and is dependent on whether the death was sudden or after long illness, the closeness of the relationship and subsequent support available.

Causes: Loss of close relationship.

Symptoms and signs: Sense of shock, numbness, grief, guilt, depression, behavioural problems, disturbed sleep, and self-injurious behaviour.

Complications: Include prolonged bereavement reaction, depressive illness, and severe behavioural disturbance.

Treatment: Support from others, and counselling are the mainstay of appropriate management, mild tranquillisers can help sleep and any disturbed behaviour.

Personality and behavioural traits: Many individuals with Down syndrome have a number of particular traits in common.

Causes: Part of the 'makeup' of adults with Down syndrome.

Symptoms and signs: The most widely known behavioural characteristics are being happy, gentle and good. A minority however are stubborn and resistant to change. Some prefer a set routine and like things in a given order, to the extent of being excessively tidy. Others also hoard items, particularly paper.

Investigation: Exclude psychological illness (eg depression, obsessive-compulsive disorder, autism – below).

Complications: Can lead to social difficulties.

Treatment: Understanding and acceptance of traits. Positive rewards to encourage desirable behaviour and behaviour modification to reduce unwanted behaviours.

Delirium: State of acute confusion. More common in the elderly.

Causes: Can be caused by many disorders including a physical illness, infections, high fever, side effects of drugs, drug toxicity, metabolic disturbances, and epilepsy (chapter 12).

Symptoms and signs: Confusion, clouding of awareness, anxiety, restlessness, mood swings, illusions (misinterpretation of real objects eg sees spots on curtains as spiders), hallucinations (experience of something being present when not there in reality eg feeling of spiders crawling over body but no spiders present), bizarre ideas, violence, and inattention. Worse at night.

Investigations: Investigations for underlying cause, including blood screen, evidence of urine infection, drug levels or more intensive tests (eg a brain scan).

Complications: Injuries. Secondary to underlying cause. If not treated may prove to be fatal.

Treatment: Treat underlying cause, reduce anxiety, ensure clear lighting, maintain fluid intake, may require admission to hospital and tranquillising medication (eg chlorpromazine, haloperidol).

Depression: Psychological condition of persistently feeling sad with loss of interest. Most people feel mildly depressed at times during their lives, often as a reaction to a situation but this is usually short-lived.

Causes: Often no apparent reason. Can commonly be a result of the loss of close person, presence of a physical illness, major life change, side-effects of medication.

Symptoms and signs: Depressed mood, loss of interest, reduced energy, tiredness, weight loss or gain, disturbed sleep pattern, reduced activity or agitation, negative thoughts, guilt, poor concentration, disturbed memory, diminished appetite, decline in social skills, occasionally thoughts of self-harm, loss of confidence, behavioural problems, delusions (irrational ideas eg postman trying to poison them) and hallucinations (experience of something being present when not there in reality eg feeling of spiders crawling over body but no spiders present). Episodes may reoccur or be associated with episodes of feeling ‘high’. Physical complaints (eg abdominal pain, stopping of periods) can occur. Decline in day-to-day self-care skills and social skills will occur.

Investigations: Differentiate from a physical problem eg hypothyroidism or from some other psychological problem eg bereavement, dementia (below).

Complications: Include injury to others, self-harm, neglect, and deterioration in physical health. There is an increased risk of further episodes.

Treatment: Need to manage any underlying factor. Can treat the depressive illness with behavioural therapy, counselling, and/or a course of antidepressants (group of drugs used to treat depression, for example amitriptyline, fluoxetine, lofepramine). Electro-convulsive therapy (ECT – form of treatment using seizures induced by electric shocks) can be administered for severe cases. Individuals may not fully recover to previous level of abilities.

Dementia (Alzheimer's disease): Dementia is a syndrome resulting from a disturbance of brain function, usually chronic and progressive in which there is deterioration in memory, thinking, comprehension, language and learning. Other features present include emotional change, deterioration in social behaviour and physical health.

Cause: For the Down syndrome population dementia is virtually always the cause of the Alzheimer's disease type. This is a form of dementia associated with large amounts of amyloid deposits (starch-like material) throughout the brain and neurofibrillary tangles (strands of protein) seen within the brain cells. The average age of onset of dementia is in the fifth decade but can begin as early as the third decade. Risk increases with age. Other causes of 'reversible' dementia include hypothyroidism (chapter 15), depression (above), a physical illness, vitamin deficiency and due to side-effects of medication.

Symptoms and signs: In the initial phase: memory impairment, disorientation in time, personality change, reduced speech output, apathy, inattention and reduced social interactions. Later problems include loss of self-help skills such as dressing, toileting, feeding, walking often slowed and shuffling, hallucinations (experience of something being present when not there in reality) and delusions (irrational ideas) possible. Late stage dementia is characterised by inability to walk, being bed-ridden, incontinent, having a flexed posture, stiffness, seizures.

Investigations: It is important to assess for causes of decline other than dementia: for example is the decline part of 'normal' ageing'? Is there a physical cause eg delirium, medication effects, brain tumour, hypothyroidism? Or a psychological cause eg depression, bereavement, change in residence? Recent evidence would suggest that doctors can test for particular genes (apolipoprotein E genes) which influence the risk of a person developing Alzheimer's disease.

Complications: Include wandering, accidents, depression (above), and epilepsy (chapter 12). Life-expectancy is significantly reduced. Dementia usually leads to death within 5–10 years after the onset of memory loss.

Treatment: There is a need for management by a specialist with knowledge of dementia in adults with learning disability. Need to maintain a familiar environment and the daily routine as long as possible. Treat any underlying cause eg hypothyroidism, depression. Treat particular problems eg poor sleep, behavioural problems with medication or behavioural therapy. Carer support is essential to reduce stress experienced by carers. May involve just giving a simple explanation of the condition or by giving more practical support (eg home help). Social services, community nurses and carer organisations are important sources of help and support. Assess risk of accidents in home eg fires, kitchen utensils. Mark coat with name and address in case of wandering. If transfer to a nursing or residential unit is necessary the situation needs to be handled with sensitivity and understanding. Recently donepezil (Aricept), rivastigamine (Exelon) and galantamine (Reminyl) are drugs which have been licensed to treat Alzheimer's disease in the general population. These drugs enhance one of the chemicals (acetylcholine) in the brain. Benefit for people with Down syndrome who have dementia and who have been treated with these drugs has been reported.

Anxiety disorders: Can be a panic attack (periodic episodes of severe anxiety which is not restricted to a particular situation – sudden intense panic) or of a generalized anxiety type (persistent anxiety not restricted to any one situation).

Causes: No one particular factor. Combination of genetic makeup from parents, personality and environment is important. Individuals with autism are more susceptible to attacks.

Symptoms and signs: Numerous features including unpleasant feeling, fear of dying, feeling of being unreal, nervousness, dizziness, choking, sweating, trembling, palpitations, muscular tension, stomach discomfort, diarrhoea, behavioural disturbance, hyperactivity, irritability, aggression, looking strained and tense, over-breathing.

Investigations: Need to screen for physical disorders eg hyperthyroidism or hypoglycaemia (chapter 15). Assess for depression (above) and ensure symptoms are not due to side-effects of medication or as part of medication withdrawal. Determine type of anxiety disorder.

Complications: Include depression, injuries (self or others), and behavioural problems.

Treatment and prevention: Reassurance, counselling, relaxation, and behavioural therapy can have a beneficial effect. Medication (mild tranquillisers, beta-blockers, antidepressants) can be prescribed but should be done under supervision and for a limited period only. Support and advice for carers is an important part of management.

Phobias: Condition where severe anxiety is provoked by a well-defined situation or object. Factors are often avoided or dreaded. Contemplation of factors can lead to anxiety. Specific phobias include heights, thunder and animals.

Causes/Symptoms and signs/Investigations/Complications/Treatment: (See anxiety disorders above).

Obsessive-compulsive disorder (OCD): Recurrent persistent thoughts (obsessions) or repetitive rituals (compulsive acts). Thoughts may be ideas, images, or impulses. Acts are behaviours repeated again and again. Distressing, the person is unable to resist and feels compelled to repeat thoughts and/or actions. Condition often chronic.

Causes: Often unknown. Can be associated with anxiety and depression.

Symptoms and signs: Commonly include repetitive thoughts, compulsive acts of washing, cleaning, checking, tidiness, and excessive ordering. If the person tries to resist he/she becomes anxious. Serious disruption in day-to-day living occurs. Can spend hours on the same compulsion.

Investigations: Differentiate from repetitive behaviours associated with learning disability or behaviours which are part of the characteristics of Down syndrome (hiding things, putting objects in the same place). Need to exclude an associated depressive illness or dementia (above).

Complications: Can lead to depression. Considerable carer stress can occur.

Treatment: Behavioural therapy, antidepressants (especially clomipramine, fluoxetine) can be of benefit but outcome is often poor. Carer support remains an important part of the management plan.

Mania/Hypomania: Psychological condition with disturbance of mood and associated overactivity, elation or irritability.

Causes: Often no obvious cause. Can be secondary to treatment with antidepressants or following environmental stress. A family history of illness may be present.

Symptoms and signs: Many features including elevated or irritable mood, increased energy and activity, sleep disturbance, excessive talking, overactivity, sexual indiscretions, distractibility, feelings of well-being, and overfamiliarity. Disruption in daily-living skills usually occurs. Hallucinations (experience of something being present when not) and delusions (irrational ideas) can occur. Aggression and behavioural deterioration is not uncommon.

Investigations: Screen for medical condition eg hyperthyroidism, delirium state. Differentiate from other mental disorders eg schizophrenia, dementia.

Complications: Physical injury or involvement in criminal behaviour can occur.

Treatment and prevention: Hospital care may be necessary. Tranquillising medication eg chlorpromazine, haloperidol may be required. Prevention of future relapse may be possible with long-term therapy with lithium or carbamazepine medication.

Schizophrenia: Uncommon condition and difficult to diagnose in people with learning disability. Is a form of mental illness characterised by disturbance in thinking, emotion and behaviour. Condition usually present for longer than 6 months. Recurrent episodes can occur leading to chronic ill health.

Causes: Often unknown.

Symptoms and signs: Commonly include personality change, hallucinations (experience of something being present when not), delusions (irrational ideas), incoherent thought, disturbance of mood, abnormal behaviour, social isolation and impairment of self-care skills. A feeling that others are sharing their thoughts, feelings or actions may be expressed by more able individuals. Can be a slow insidious onset. Recurrent episodes may lead to 'negative state' of marked apathy, reduced speech, flat emotions, and social withdrawal. Predominant symptoms may include marked paranoid ideas (abnormal ideas of persecution), aggression or deterioration in behaviour.

Investigations: Assess for other causes of confusion eg delirious state, epilepsy, depression, mania.

Complications: Can become a chronic condition. Recurrent relapses are common. Injury to self or to others can occur. Can lead to criminal offences eg fire-setting, assaults on others.

Treatment: May require treatment in hospital. Antipsychotic medication (eg chlorpromazine, haloperidol) often required. Support for family and carers is important. Voluntary support groups are available. Compliance with medication is important to prevent a future relapse. Behavioural therapy can have a limited benefit. Ongoing community rehabilitation is necessary for chronic cases.

Autism: In strict terms autism is classified as a 'developmental problem' rather than as a 'psychological disorder'. However it will be discussed here due to the major psychological problems associated with the condition. This condition is associated with significant problems in social interaction, communication and restricted repetitive behaviour manifested at early age (usually before 3 years). Not accountable for by the underlying learning disability.

Causes: Generally unknown although many unproven theories have been proposed. Possible factors are personality, chemical changes in brain, diet, family or environment factors.

Investigations: Need to differentiate from behaviours associated with learning disability, hearing or visual impairment, and from emotional problems eg depression, obsessive compulsive disorder (above).

Symptoms and signs: Impaired social interaction (lack of response to others, impaired play activity, make-believe). Poor language expression and conversation, lack of gestures. Restricted repertoire of activities and interests, repetitive behaviour, rigid routine. Preoccupation with dates, routes, timetables. Resistance to change. Other problems include fears or phobias, sleep and eating problems, aggression, and temper tantrums.

Complications: Increased risk of seizures or depression.

Treatment: Behavioural therapy and carer support are the mainstay of management. Medication for some behaviours can be used eg propranolol for anxiety attacks.

Hyperkinetic Disorder (Attention Deficit Disorder [ADD]): Strictly speaking a hyperkinetic disorder is a disorder of development rather than of the mind. However there is a major emotional aspect to the disorder as well as involving difficulties in behaviour. The disorder may be under-reported due to difficulty in distinguishing the disorder from mental age related overactivity or from autism.

Causes: (See autism above).

Symptoms and signs: Overactive, fidgetiness, distractibility, impatience, inattentiveness, impulsivity, failure to complete activities. Inability to follow instructions, poor listening. Can lead to unpopularity and behavioural problems.

Investigations: Differentiate from other behavioural disorders, mood or anxiety problems.

Complications: Behavioural problems can persist. Injuries to self or others.

Treatment: Behavioural therapy often with home and daycare involved, avoid overstimulation. Psycho-stimulant drugs which stimulate the mind (eg Ritalin) can be used but under close medical supervision.

APPENDICES AND RESOURCES

Appendix A

MEDICAL CHECK LIST

More so than for the general population it is most important that individuals with Down syndrome receive the usual healthcare screening procedures and have regular healthcare check-ups to detect any possible illness. This applies to all ages of adults with Down syndrome.

Below is a check list summarizing the health issues, discussed in earlier chapters, which should be routinely assessed in adults with Down syndrome. A detailed medical history and a detailed physical and psychological examination are the basis of a good health assessment. Particular attention should be given to some of the problems listed below. **If health problems occur then a medical opinion should always be considered.**

Particular problems for carers to watch out for:

obesity
decline in vision
loss of hearing
dental problems
delayed sexual development
problems with menstruation
heart failure
behavioural difficulties
sleep apnoea

depression
dementia
seizures

Particular areas of health for professionals to observe:

weight
eyes (visual acuity, cataracts, keratoconus)
ears (hearing loss)
heart murmur
sexual awareness development
menstrual cycle
epilepsy
dental hygiene
thyroid disease
depression
dementia
behavioural difficulties
medication

Routine checks carers and professionals should be aware of:

measure weight at least once a year
vision every 1–2 years
hearing every 1–2 years
teeth every 1–2 years
thyroid function tests every 2–3 years
blood screen every 2–3 years
breast examination monthly
echocardiogram if heart murmur develops (exclude mitral valve prolapse)
psychological status every 1–2 years
review of medication every year

Areas of further intervention by carers and professionals:

education regarding health issues
advice regarding particular health issues eg dental care, obesity, hypothyroidism, epilepsy
parent/carer support groups
recreational/vocational programs
self-advocacy
sex education
consent issues
how to access health and social services
available residential facilities
bereavement counselling for those who experience loss

Appendix B

FURTHER READING AND SOURCES OF INFORMATION

A Practical Guide for Disabled People: Where to find information, services and equipment. Free copies from: Department of Health, P0 Box 410, Wetherby, L523

Alzheimer Disease, Down Syndrome, and Their Relationship. (1993). Berg, J.M., Karlinsky, H., Holland, A.J. Oxford Medical Publications, Oxford.

Benefits and Services for People with Hearing Loss/Deaf and Hard of Hearing People: Basic Introduction to Deafness and Some of the surrounding issues/The Facts about Hearing Loss Royal National Institute for Deaf People, London

Biomedical Concerns in Persons with Down Syndrome. (1992). Pueschel, S.M. and Pueschel, J.K. Paul H. Brookes Publishing Co.

Dentistry for Special Needs (1995) Bedi, R. and Pollard, D. For IBM 386/486 or compatibles running Windows. The School of Dentistry, University of Birmingham

Down Syndrome. Living and Learning in the Community (1995) Nadel, L. and Rosenthal. WileyLiss Inc

Down Syndrome – Advances in medical care (1992) Lott, I.T. and McCoy, E.E. Wiley-Liss Inc

Down Syndrome. Advances in Biomedicine and the Behavioural Sciences. (1982). Pueschel, S.M. and Rynders, J.E. Academic Guild Publishers.

Down Syndrome. The Facts. (1997). Selikowitz, M. Oxford University Press, Oxford.

Down's Syndrome. Psychological, Psychobiological and Socio-educational Perspectives. (1996). Rondal, J.A., Perera, J., Nadel, L and Comblain, A. Whurr Publishers Ltd.

Down's Syndrome, Children Growing Up. (1995). Carr, J. Cambridge University Press.

Down's Anomaly (1976). Smith, G.F. and Berg, J.M. Longnian Group Ltd.

Going to the Doctor (1996). Hollins S., Bernal J. and Gregory, M., St George's Mental Health Library, London.

Good Practice in Breast and Cervical Screening for Women with Learning Disabilities. (2000). NHSCSP Publications, Sheffield.

Health Care Guidelines for Individuals with Down Syndrome 1999 Revision. Cohen, W.I. Down Syndrome Quarterly, 4, no 3, September.

How to Use your Hearing Aid (HA G2) Department of Health. PO Box 410, Wetherby, L523 7LN.

Keep Yourself Healthy: A Guide to Checking your Breasts. Family Advice and Information Resource Centre. 25–27 West Nicolson Street, Edinburgh, EH8 9DB.

Keeping Healthy Down Below. (2001). Hollins, S. and Downer, J. Gaskell and St George's Hospital.

Looking After My Breasts. (2001). Hollins, S., Perez, W., Gaskell Press and St George's Hospital.

Mental Handicap & Sexuality: Issues and Perspectives. Craft. Costello Publishers Ltd.

New Approaches to Down Syndrome. (1996). Eds. Stratford, B. and Gunn, P. Casell, London.

New Perspectives on Down Syndrome. (1987). Pueschel, S., Tingley, C., Rynders, J., Crocker, A., and Crutcher, D. Paul H. Brookes Publishing Co.

Now They're Growing Up: Booklets for Parents. Shepherd School Sex Education Monitoring Group. David Stewart. Shepherd School, Nottingham. NG8 3BB.

Primary Care for People with a Mental Handicap. (1990). Occasional Paper 47. London: Royal College of General Practitioners.

Sexual Health Education. Children and Young People with Learning Disabilities – A Practical Way of Working. (1996). Adcock, K. and Stanley, G. BILD Publications, Kidderminster.

Sexuality and People with Intellectual Disability. (1993). Fegan. L., Rauch, A., and McCarthy, W. London. Maclennan and Petty.

Sport and Leisure: An In Touch Care Guide. BBC, In Touch Publishing, 37 Charles Street, Cardiff CFl 4EB

Teenage Years. A Sex Education Handbook for Parents. Mrs Banks/Mr Sterling, Cromwell Senior School. Stockport.

Ten Things You Should Know about Visual Impairment. Royal National Institute for the Blind, London.

The Adolescent with Down's Syndrome. (1987). Buckley and Sacks. Portsmouth Down's Syndrome Trust.

The Fulton Special Education Digest. Selected Resources for Teachers, Parents and Carers. (1999). Worthington, A. (ed). David Fulton, London.

The Down's Syndrome Handbook. (1997). Newton, R. Vermilion.

The Health of the Nation: A Strategy for People with Learning Disabilities Department of Health. P0 Box 410, Wetherby

The Sexuality and Sexual Rights of People with Learning Disabilities. (1996). Cambridge, P.

Plymouth: BILD Publications, Green Street, Kidderminster, Worcs DY10 1JL.

You, Your Body and Sex. Mistgrove Ltd Box 2127 London.

Your Good Health (1998) Harris, J. and Simpson, N. BILD Publications, Green Street, Kidderminster, Worcs DY10 1JL.

Your Rights about Sex. (1996). McCarthy, M and Cambridge. P. Plymouth: BILD Publications, Green Street, Kidderminster, Worcs DY10 1JL. A booklet for people with learning disabilities.

Appendix C

USEFUL ADDRESSES, TELEPHONE NUMBERS AND WEB SITES

United Kingdom

Alzheimer's Disease Society
Gordon House
10 Green Coat Place
London SW1P 1PH
Tel: Helpline 0845 3000 336

British Dietetic Association
5th Floor, Charles House,
148/149 Great Charles Street
Queensway, Birmingham B33 HT
Tel: 0121 200 8080

British Institute of Learning Disabilities (BILD)
Campion House
Green Street
Kidderminster
Worcestershire DY10 1JL

The British Sports Association for the Disabled,
Box Hill Centre, Boxhill Road, Harold Hill,
Essex
Tel: 01708 377648

Brook Advisory Centre,
153a East Street,
London, SEl 7 *25D*
Tel: Helpline 0800 0185 023

Carers' National Association
20/25 Glasshouse Yard
London ECIA 4J5
Tel: Carers Line 0207 490 8898

Council for Disabled Children
8 Wakely Street,
London, ECIV 7QE.
Tel: 0207 843 6000

Disability, Sport England (DSE)
13 Brunswick Place
London NI 6DX
Tel: 0207 490 4919

Down's Heart Group
17 Cantilupe Close
Eaton Bray
Dunstable, Beds LU6 2EA
Tel: 0152 522 0379

Down's Syndrome Association
155 Mitcham Road,
London, SWl7 9PG
Tel: 0208 682 4001

Down Syndrome Educational Trust
The Sarah Duffen Centre
Belmont Street, Southsea, P05 lNA.
Tel: 023 9282 4261

MENCAP
123 Golders Lane,
London EC1Y ORT
Tel: 0207 454 0454; Helpline 0808 808 111

NAPSAC (National Association for the Protection from Sexual Abuse of Adults and Children with Learning Disabilities). The Department of Mental Handicap, University Hospital, Nottingham NG7 2UH
Tel: 0115 924 9924

National Deaf Children's Society
15 Dufferin Street,
London, EC1Y 8UR
Free line: 0808 800 8880

PHAB Ltd
Summitt House, 50 Wandle Road,
Croydon, Surrey, CR0 1DF
Tel: 020 8667 9443

Riding for the Disabled Association
Lavinia Norfolk House, Avenue R, National Agricultural Centre
Stoneleigh Park
Warwickshire CV8 2LY
Tel: 024 7669 6510

Royal National Institute for the Blind (RNTB)
224 St Portland Street, London W1M 6AA
Tel: 0171 388 1266

Royal National Institute for the Deaf (RNID)
19-23 Featherstone Street, London EClY 8FL
Tel: 0207 296 8000

Speakeasy (The Association of Speech Impaired)
Pentne Farm, Pentne,
Bucknell, Shropshire SY7 0BU
Tel: 01547 520 332

SPOD (Association to Aid the Sexual and Personal Relationships of People with a Disability)
286 Camden Road,
London, N7 OBI
Tel: 0207 607 8851; Helpline 020 7607 9191

The Law Society's Group for the Welfare of People with a Handicap
117–123 Golden Lane, London, EC1Y ORT.
Tel: 0207 242 1222

The Partially Sighted Society
9 Plato Place, 72–74 St Dionis Road,
London SW6 4TU
Tel: 0207 371 0289

The Scottish Down's Syndrome Association
158–160 Balgreen Road
Edinburgh
EH11 3AU
Tel: 0131 313 4225

United Kingdom Sports Association for People with Learning Disability
Leroy House, 436 Essex Road,
London N1 3QP
Tel: 0207 354 1030

Europe

European Down Syndrome Association
Rue V Close, 41 B-4800
Polleur Verviers
Belgium
Tel: 3287 22335/228833

Ireland

Down's Syndrome Ireland
41 Lower Dominick Street
Dublin 1
Ireland

United States of America

National Down Syndrome Society
666 Broadway, New York,
NY 10012-2317
USA

National Down Syndrome Congress
1605 Chantilly Drive, Suite 250
Atlanta
GA 30324-3269
USA

USEFUL WEB SITES:

Down Syndrome Association
http://www.downs-syndrome.org.uk/

Down Syndrome Educational Trust
http://www.downsnet.org

National Down Syndrome Society
http://www.ndss.org

The Down's heart group
http://www.downs-heart.downsnet.org

Down syndrome quarterly journal
http://www.denison.edu/dsq

Down syndrome research and practice journal
http://www.downsnet.org/drsp/issues_contents.asp

Web-based information for medical students and other health professionals
http://www.intellectualdisability.info

Down Syndrome Medical Interest Group (DSMIG)
http://www.dsmig.org.uk

UK resources for Down's syndrome
http://www.43green.freeserve.co.uk

Index